CONTENTS

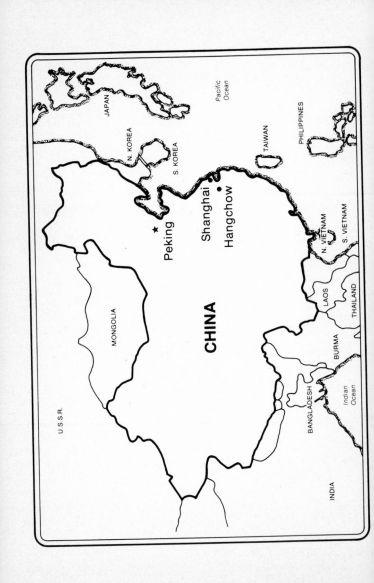

"This was the
week that
changed the world."
—Richard M. Nixon

THE PRESIDENT'S TRIP TO CHINA

TEXT

EDITOR, RICHARD WILSON,
DES MOINES REGISTER & TRIBUNE SYNDICATE

WRITERS: CHARLES BAILEY, MINNEAPOLIS TRIBUNE
ROBERT S. BOYD, KNIGHT NEWSPAPERS
STAN CARTER, NEW YORK DAILY NEWS
BOB CONSIDINE, HEARST NEWSPAPERS
FRANK CORMIER, ASSOCIATED PRESS
ROBERT KEATLEY, WALL STREET JOURNAL
PHILIP POTTER, BALTIMORE SUN
R. H. SHACKFORD, SCRIPPS-HOWARD
JERRY TERHORST, DETROIT NEWS
HELEN THOMAS, UNITED PRESS INTERNATIONAL
RICHARD WILSON

PHOTOGRAPHS

OLLIE ATKINS, PERSONAL PHOTOGRAPHER
TO PRESIDENT RICHARD M. NIXON
BYRON SHUMAKER, WHITE HOUSE PHOTOGRAPHER

The President's Trip to China

A pictorial record
of the historic journey to
the People's Republic of China
with text by members
of the American Press Corps

BANTAM BOOKS
NEW YORK • LONDON • TORONTO

A NATIONAL GENERAL COMPANY

THE PRESIDENT'S TRIP TO CHINA
A Bantam Book / published March 1972

Published simultaneously in the United States and Canada

Bantam Books are published by Bantam Books, Inc., a National
General company. Its trade-mark, consisting of the words "Bantam
Books" and the portrayal of a bantam, is registered in the United
States Patent Office and in other countries. Marca Registrada.
Bantam Books, Inc., 666 Fifth Avenue, New York, N.Y. 10019.

PRINTED IN THE UNITED STATES OF AMERICA

INTRODUCTION

BY PHILIP POTTER

The United States and the People's Republic of China are now in communication, and President Nixon, back from an eight-day visit to China and talks with its Communist leaders, has a piece of paper to prove it.

The paper, the President surely hopes, will be a political coup in this election year, a proof that he is making good on his pledge of a "generation of peace."

But it could also be his Yalta, as politically damaging to the Republicans as the accord President Franklin D. Roosevelt reached with Stalin at that Soviet watering place during World War II, subsequently labeled by then-Congressman Nixon and other GOP members of Congress as a Democratic giveaway that "lost China."

Mr. Nixon, the nemesis of Alger Hiss, was as vigorous as any, up to at least 1960, in warning against any pandering to the "international criminals" in Peking. This was his theme in many a speech directed at Senator John F. Kennedy as the two men fought for the presidency.

Loser in the election, Mr. Nixon turned to law, often traveling in Asia on behalf of clients. It may have changed his views about the Mao Tse-tung regime in Peking. As early as 1967, he was considering a trip to Communist China with the Prime Minister of Newfoundland and Labrador, and writing in *Foreign Affairs* that China should not remain forever isolated from American contact.

As President-elect in November 1968, he accepted a public proposal by Peking on the 26th of that month for resumption of the Warsaw ambassadorial talks, which had been suspended since January 8 of that year. The only direct link between Washington and Peking, they had been held on and off since 1955.

American diplomats were interested at the time in Peking's invitation for a discussion in Warsaw over a possible agreement on the "five principles of peaceful coexistence."

Some saw in it a Peking turning moderate after Red Guard radicalism in the Cultural Revolution of 1966–67.

The Warsaw meeting was scheduled for February 1969, but was canceled because of a dispute over a Chinese defector in the Netherlands to whom the United States promised asylum.

Mr. Nixon, however, quietly went ahead with efforts to establish a dialogue with leaders of the Chinese People's Republic.

In Paris, on March 1, 1969, he solicited help from President Charles de Gaulle in transmitting to Peking his desire to move toward normalization of relations.

High American officials, meanwhile, voiced hopes for contacts with the Mao regime, and Mr. Nixon ordered removal of some restrictions on trade with and travel to China. More were lifted later.

On December 3, 1969, Walter J. Stoessel, Jr., American ambassador to Poland, met formally with Lei Yang, the Chinese chargé d'affaires, in the first direct contact with China since Mr. Nixon took office.

On February 20, 1970, in an hour-long meeting at the United States embassy in Warsaw, Ambassador Stoessel told Mr. Lei that the President would like to send a senior administration official to Peking.

It was not until fourteen months later in April 1971, however, that Peking said yes. And in July, Henry A. Kissinger was received in the Chinese capital for long talks with Premier Chou En-lai, slipping in secretly through Pakistan.

On his return came the July 15 announcement that Mr. Nixon had accepted an invitation to visit China "at an appropriate date before May 1972."

There followed another trip to China by the President's adviser on national security in October, and soon thereafter an American official advance party was sent in and the February 21–28 trip was set up.

It was on October 10, 1949, that Mao proclaimed the existence of the People's Republic of China, having tamed Chiang Kai-shek's forces in a civil war that began after Japan's surrender in World War II.

During that world war, the U.S. put 70,000 military men into China to train Chiang's troops to use American weaponry flown across the Himalayas, and to fly bombing missions against Japan and its forces in China. For a brief period, relations with Mao's Communist guerrilla forces were good.

Some State Department officials sensed in Mao's leadership and the character of his military forces the wave of the future in China.

Some were later pilloried by Senator Joseph McCarthy of Wisconsin and purged during the Eisenhower regime by Secretary of State John Foster Dulles.

Dulles, while in Geneva in 1954 for the conference that divided up Indochina after the French disaster at Dienbienphu, turned up by several notches the ill-feeling between China's government and our own. At a chance meeting with Premier Chou in a conference hall, Mr. Dulles spurned a proffered handshake, a snub the Premier has often complained about to visiting journalists.

President Nixon finally made up for it on arriving in Peking with hand outstretched on February 21, 1972.

American-Chinese relations were sour, however, even before Mr. Dulles added vinegar.

At the end of World War II, President Truman sent General George C. Marshall to China to halt a burgeoning civil war, to bring the Communists into a coalition government, and their forces into an integrated nationalist army.

He secured some agreements for cease-fires, but deep mistrust thwarted the effort.

Chou En-lai, who did the negotiating for Mao, was enraged by the U.S. sale of war-surplus weapons to Chiang's government. He accused the mediator of "hypocrisy."

The American general, his task obviously hopeless, was withdrawn in January 1947.

In less than three years the Communists had conquered China, destroying Chiang's armies, which had been carried to Manchuria by American air- and sealift.

Chiang fled with troops and treasure to Taiwan.

When the People's Republic of China came into being in 1949, President Truman considered recognition, despite a chorus of dissent from top-ranking Republicans in Congress. They clearly sensed political pay dirt in laying the "loss" of China to a Democratic administration.

The Mao regime itself made recognition difficult by arresting American consuls and demanding tribute for exit visas given American businessmen whose properties were sequestered.

President Truman, in January 1950, formally stated that the U.S. would not intervene in China's civil war, even to the extent of furnishing military "aid or advice" to Chiang's regime on Formosa (Taiwan).

He arranged to put the "China question" on the agenda of the United Nations, opening the way to Peking's claim for the China seats in the General Assembly and Security Council.

But UN entry and American diplomatic relations with Peking became moot in 1950 when General Douglas MacArthur sent troops of his United Nations command across the 38th Parallel in Korea, after turning back an invasion of the South by the Communist forces of Kim Il-Sung in North Korea.

Peking fired a warning to the U.S. to stay away from the Yalu River, constituting the China-Korea border, and sent so-called "volunteers" into battle when the warning went unheeded.

President Truman responded by sending the U.S. 7th Fleet into the Taiwan straits and began supplying Chiang's forces with weapons and advice.

Bloody fighting between Chinese and American forces ensued in Korea until an armistice was signed in 1953, fulfilling Eisenhower's promise to end the war if elected President.

He claimed in a book that a threat to use atomic weapons was an inducement for Peking to accept a cease-fire. China's manpower losses to American firepower had already been enormous.

China removed its last troops from North Korea in 1958. It has demanded since that the U.S. get its military out of the South, too.

The French downfall in Indochina brought new fear in

Washington of Chinese hegemonial ambitions in Southeast Asia.

To meet it, Mr. Dulles framed the Southeast Asia Treaty Organization.

In a fast journey through Southeast Asia in spring of 1955, he assured Thais, Laotians, Cambodians, South Vietnamese, and Filipinos that SEATO and a "mosaic" of American defense pacts with Japan, South Korea, Australia, and New Zealand would assure their protection against further Communist encroachments.

American sea and air power, he said, would be the U.S. contribution and would be enough. Occasionally, American nuclear weapons were brandished by American commanders in the Pacific as crises in East Asia arose.

Chou En-lai contrived with India's Prime Minister Nehru in 1954 the "five principles of peaceful coexistence," and at the Asian-African conference in Bandung in April 1955, sold at least some East Asian nations on the idea that China was no threat.

He also made a bid for direct talks with the U.S. on the critical Formosa issue, disclaimed any desire for war with America, and suggested negotiations to discuss the relaxation of tensions in the Far East, particularly Taiwan.

It led to the Warsaw talks. But neither party came to grips with the Formosa problem, the U.S. insisting that Chiang must participate in any such discussion "as an equal," and Premier Chou asserting China's "sovereign right to liberate the island" as solely an internal problem.

The Warsaw talks solved little beyond the repatriation of Americans trying to get out of China and of Chinese trying to get out of the United States to work for the Communist regime, including some of Mao's best atomic physicists.

In 1958, when the Peking regime made threatening moves toward the Nationalist offshore islands, the U.S. sent warships to convoy the Generalissimo's troops and weapons to Quemoy and Matsu, and the Peking regime backed off.

The early 1960s brought little change in the estrangement between the U.S. and China, and American involvement in Vietnam deepened it.

Then came Mr. Nixon, with a program for sharp reduction of American forces in Indochina, approaches to China through secret intermediaries, and the results as indicated above.

As the President says, there still is a "long road" to travel before normal diplomatic relations are established with the Chinese People's Republic. But the journey has begun.

THE FLIGHT TO CHINA

BY FRANK CORMIER

Superstitious Chinese of pre-Liberation days might have thought it an omen, but to Americans it was an interesting coincidence: Richard M. Nixon left Washington on his 11,510-mile flight to China in thirty-four degree weather and, four days later, reached Peking with the thermometer registering an identical reading.

The President and Mrs. Nixon boarded *Air Force One,* recently renamed *The Spirit of '76,* in an ebullient mood. Within minutes of takeoff from Andrews Air Force Base in suburban Maryland, they walked through the Boeing 707, shaking hands and chatting with most of the fifty-two others aboard. Trailing her husband, Pat Nixon insisted, "I can't let my old man get ahead of me."

One of seven reporters and photographers on the smooth-flying jet handed the Chief Executive an elaborate China atlas with the credit "Central Intelligence Agency" on the cover.

"Do you think they'll let us in with this?" Nixon was asked.

"This will probably show how much we don't know about China," he countered.

The President proudly stated that, because of his travels to seventy-six countries, a dozen of them in Asia, he needed no practice in the use of chopsticks. "But," he said, pointing to his wife, "she does." He had to be joking. She later proved to be qualified for an expert badge.

The big plane was piloted by graying, forty-seven-year-old Ralph Albertazzie, a "bird colonel" straight out of the

Steve Canyon comic strip. To him, landing in Peking, China, was no different than going to Pekin, Illinois. He'd been there before with the first advance party headed by Henry A. Kissinger, principal architect of the President's China visit.

Serving the President and First Lady were Senior Master Sergeant James Brown of McFarland, California, and Master Sergeant Russell Reid of Morganton, South Carolina. Helping were Master Sergeant Harry Formby of Raleigh, North Carolina, and Technical Sergeant James Hames of Gaffney, South Carolina.

Food for the round-trip flight was prepared in air force kitchens at Andrews and placed in the jet's hold in dry ice. The Nixons did not have to eat the set meals, however. An ample supply of cottage cheese and catsup was available in the forward galley, close by the three-room presidential suite.

Sixteen men manned the plane. Four were air force security policemen: once in China it was their assignment to mount a twenty-four hour watch around the craft. Chinese guards helped them.

No one on board could forget the destination. Chopsticks were provided at the first two airborne meals. The White House signaled its total preoccupation with the journey by having a red rose placed on the meal trays served to the women making the trip.

In effect, the President transformed his plane into a flying foreign-policy command post. For twenty-three hours and twenty minutes, *The Spirit of '76* was the nation's nerve center. Popping in and out of the Nixon suite were Secretary of State William P. Rogers and Kissinger. Through the plane's sophisticated communications gear, the President and his aides were as close to the world as the nearest of the multiple telephones on the big blue, white, and silver bird.

First stop was the Marine Corps Air Station at Kaneohe Bay in Hawaii. The President borrowed the seventeen-room house of a marine general which commanded a spectacular view of the sea and nearby islands.

Leaving Kaneohe, Nixon told the hundreds who came to see him off, "Tomorrow I will be in China. I think it is most appropriate that this journey begins in Hawaii—a state where East and West really do meet."

Nixon paced his journey with the hope of adjusting to the physiological and psychological effects of flying across many time zones and the international date line at jet speed. After a day and a half on Oahu, the chief executive stopped on Guam—"Where America's Day Begins"—for an overnight stop before flying into China.

En route, he again toured the plane and chatted with the small press contingent aboard. He reported that he tested Hawaii's surf but "the waves were so big I almost got rolled."

In Shanghai we were to take aboard nine Chinese crewmen, including a navigator and radio operator for the short hop to Peking. (The Chinese crewmen were reputed to be fluent in English, but the navigator, at least, had to rely on earthbound air controllers to translate his flight deck conversations with pilot Albertazzie and the copilot, Lieutenant Colonel Carl Peden of Visalia, California.)

The Nixons' China landfall was at the Rainbow Bridge Airport in Shanghai. The time, 8:55 A.M.; the day, February 21, 1972.

PEKING

BY J. F. TERHORST

Would you believe

—The President of the United States quoting Mao Tse-tung on February 22, George Washington's birthday?

—President Nixon applauding a Chinese ballet in which Red women guerrillas used Nationalist China's President Chiang Kai-shek as a target for rifle practice?

—Richard Nixon, looking over the Great Wall of China and remarking, "This is a great wall!"

—Dick Nixon, veteran Commie-fighter, table-hopping at a Chinese banquet and exchanging toasts of fiery white brandy with a score of Peking leaders and Liberation Army generals?

Believe it.

All this and more comprised the mind-boggling tableau starring President Nixon during the momentous first five days of his visit to the People's Republic of China.

But then, Peking always has had its own special effect on visitors. Nearly 700 years ago, the famed Marco Polo came to Peking, then the seat of power of the Mongol invaders, and chronicled his amazement in these words: "Things . . . more strange come into this town of Cambaluc [Peking] than into any city of the world. . . . Everyone from everywhere brings there for the lord who lives there and for his court."

Peking's current lord, Party Chairman Mao, god-figure of the Chinese Communist revolution, recently supplied a new thought to justify the arrival of President Nixon, hitherto the most reviled leader of western "imperialism:"

"Affairs in the world require consultations. . . . They must not be decided [only] by the two big powers."

Peking, from Kublai Khan to Mao Tse-tung, draws the past and present and the power of China together with magnetizing force. Old palaces and pagodas, the ancient Forbidden City of the Ming and Ching dynasties, are intermixed with the red billboards and massive new buildings of Mao's Communist society.

Premier Chou En-lai was as good a host as any Ming emperor, providing everything the President could have desired by way of luxurious quarters, abundant and exotic food, servants, and scenes to please the eye and assuage the ego. But the Communist treatment of Nixon in Peking was impressive also for its isolation of Nixon from the nearly 7 million souls who live in the city and its environs. Not once did Nixon get a chance to mingle with the citizens. Not once did the Chinese government assemble the multitudes on Tienanmen Square for Nixon, as it has done on past occasions for other important guests.

Perhaps the biggest street throng Nixon saw was an army of several thousand children and soldiers that was mobilized to scrape, shovel, and sweep away the fresh fall of snow on the morning of February 24, his fourth day, outside the guest compound where he stayed. Like the snow, they melted away when the sun came out.

Nixon got his first glimpse of Peking about 11:25 A.M., Monday, February 21, when his blue and white air force jet broke through the smog from a million coal-burning chimneys and began its final approach into Peking's wind-swept airport.

"That is affirmative—no crowd," a secret service agent on the airfield radioed the curious President aboard the plane. On hand were forty-two Chinese officials headed by Chou, the Chinese army band, an honor guard of 500 soldiers, sailors, and airmen in brown fur hats and greatcoats, plus the American press corps and advance party members already in Peking to await the Nixons' arrival. There were no foreign diplomats, as is customary for the arrival of heads of countries with whom Peking maintains diplomatic relations. Except for a handful of curious airport employees, press bus drivers, and limousine chauffeurs, there were no ordinary folk at all to greet the President of the United States.

A single American flag fluttered fitfully from a tall staff, opposite one bearing the bright scarlet banner of the People's Republic of China. Between them, superimposed on the bleak stone front of the terminal building, was a gigantic color portrait of Mao. On all sides of the airfield were the big red signs bearing slogans of Chinese communism: "People of oppressed nations the world over—unite!" "Long live the great Chinese Communist Party and long live our great leader Chairman Mao." "The theoretical basis governing our thinking is Marxism-Leninism."

But crowds or no crowds, such was the high drama of the moment that when *The Spirit of '76* rolled to a stop and the door opened, onlookers fully expected to see the booted foot of an astronaut emerge from the cabin.

Instead, it was the President of the United States, hatless, accompanied by a smiling wife, who descended the red-carpeted ramp to Peking's moonscape at 11:32 A.M. (10:32 P.M. Sunday, February 20, EST).

In less than fifteen minutes, the Nixon motorcade was sweeping along the fifteen miles of open road into Peking and to his guest compound on the western outskirts. Here and there were knots of people, held back from the inter-sections by unarmed police and armed soldiers of the People's Liberation Army.

The Nixons stayed in a government guest house named Taio Yu Tai, "The Fishing Terrace." It was of nondescript Western architecture, a yellowish brick structure distin-guished mainly by empty gardens and barren willow trees framing a small frozen lake. Quartered nearby were the President's key advisers, including Dr. Henry A. Kissinger and Secretary of State William P. Rogers.

Nixon's mood, at this point, was less than exuberant. The absence of crowds seemed to signal that the leaders of China had determined to be icily correct about his visit. But in Communist China, one learns to expect the unexpected. And so it was with Nixon. The unexpected came from Premier Chou: Would the President and Kissinger like to join him at the home of the revered Chairman Mao? Nixon reacted with alacrity to the summons from China's Mount Olympus. And with much secrecy.

While the pool of American newsmen and photographers waited outside the guest house to accompany the President to a scheduled meeting with Chou at the Great Hall of the People on Tienanmen Square, Nixon and Kissinger slipped out another door and sped in a boxy "Red Flag" limousine, with drawn curtains, to Mao's residence.

It was the first and only private home the President en-tered during his week's stay in China. It was, obviously, the most important of all the homes in China. And the least known, even to the Chinese. So secretive were the Chinese officials who escorted Nixon to Mao's residence that White House News Secretary Ronald Ziegler would not describe it or its location. A member of Kissinger's staff suggested the description of the late Edgar Snow, long-time American friend of Mao:

. . . Chairman Mao's residence in Peking lies in the southwest corner of the former Forbidden City, surrounded by vermillion walls and not far from the Tienanmen or Heavenly Peace Gate where he reviews the October anniversary parade. Behind these high walls, topped by glistening yellow tiles, the old imperial regime also housed its officials.

Within the compound, no guards were visible along a willow-fringed drive that skirted the palace lakes, past beds of gladioli and chrysanthemums, to the graceful, old, one-story, yellow-roof residence. The large, comfortable living room is tastefully furnished in Chinese style; directly adjoining it are a small dining room and his study and living quarters.

The hour with Mao set the tone for the entire Nixon journey thereafter. Most immediately, it provided an upbeat mood for the big banquet Chou gave for Nixon that first night in the Great Hall of the People.

The Great Hall, dedicated to the glory of Mao and Marxism, is a Pentagon-sized structure designed as a center for all state functions of the People's Republic of China. It is situated on the west side of Tienanmen Square, where the great parades of massed millions are held on China's public holidays. The Great Hall was built in eleven months during 1958–59, the period of the Chinese Communists' Great Leap Forward. It is a handsome structure, inside and out, with pillars and grand staircases and high-ceilinged corridors leading from one reception room to another. The Great Hall houses the office of the Standing Commitee of the National People's Congress, the basic organization of the state. Premier Chou has his offices here and it was here that Nixon and Chou conducted most of their diplomatic talks. It also has an auditorium seating more than 10,000, where Communist Party congresses are held; a banquet hall which seats 5,000, and numerous large rooms decorated tastefully according to the local designs and motifs of each of China's provinces and autonomous regions. It is truly a work of the people. During each day of its construction, more than 14,000 persons from all the provinces worked feverishly on the building to meet Mao's deadline. It was the place that Nixon saw most—in meetings with Chou, two banquets, and a special performance of China's revolutionary ballet.

Downtown Peking regaled the President with two spectaculars rich in cultural counterpoint.

Picture yourself in an indoor auditorium, say Madison Square Garden or the Los Angeles Sports Arena. Paper it with 18,000 people, one section solidly military, like an Army-Navy game, but still more Chinese people than Nixon has seen in three days, in a city the size of Chicago. That was the President's pleasure the night Premier Chou escorted him to the "sports performances" at Peking Capital Stadium. The flower of Chinese gymnasts performed on the mats, the bars, the rings, and the vaulting horses. China's foremost badminton and table tennis players, probably the world's best, put on an exhibition of skill and dexterity that had the Nixons gasping with delight. The President did not miss the symbolism. After all, ping-pong diplomacy had opened the door of China in 1971 for the first time in two decades. Nor could he overlook another bit of symbolism in the manner the sports program had been opened: the precision march-on of muscular Chinese athletes, male and female, garbed in red and white. To the blare of martial trumpets, the rhythmic clapping of 18,000 Chinese in the stands, and following massed red flags, they proudly goose-stepped the length of the colosseum.

Like Marco Polo before him, Nixon could not resist the opportunity to see the fabled Forbidden City, the high-walled, moated city-within-a-city where the ancient emperors and empresses of the Ming and Ching dynasties lived, ruled, and hoarded their treasures in splendor unsurpassed anywhere in the world. The Imperial Palace, as it's now known in China, is the largest and most complete ensemble of traditional Chinese architecture. It was begun in

1406, fourth year of the reign of the Ming emperor Yung Lo. The grounds and gardens cover an area of 720,000 square meters. The Palace contains more than 9,000 rooms, decorated with fine gold, silver, jade, and precious stones, intricately carved doorways and arches and brocade tapestries of immense value. As the tourist map explains, "it is handiwork reflecting the wisdom and talents of the Chinese working people."

The Nixons were up early and warmly bundled the day they took off on the thirty-mile trip by limousine to the northwest mountains to see the Great Wall of China. The weather was sunny and cold. The wind picked up as their caravan wound up the narrow, twisting road toward the Nanku Pass in the Yenshan mountain range.

The Wall is truly one of the wonders of the world. Built more than 2,000 years ago by forced labor to keep out nomadic tribes that threatened China's security, the Wall was extended during the later Ming and Ching dynasties until it stretched diagonally for more than 3,600 miles, snaking up and down the rugged mountain ridges. Imagine a stone wall twenty-four feet high and eighteen feet wide at the top.

Nixon spent little more than twenty minutes there. Then he sped off to see the nearby Ming Tombs, vast underground palaces where the emperors and empresses of China were buried amid splendor equalling the Pharaohs of Egypt. Surveying the underground treasures in one of the tombs, Mr. Nixon discovered something familiar.

"Ah!", he exclaimed, peering into a display case featuring jewel-encrusted eating utensils. "They had spoons as well as chopsticks!"

After that, it was downhill by limousine back to Peking.

THE WORKING SIDE

BY R. H. SHACKFORD

President Nixon's summit meeting with the leaders of the People's Republic of China was unprecedented in many ways. It was the first time that an American President in office had ever visited China. More important, it was the first time that an American President had ever negotiated on the soil of a nation with which the United States did not have diplomatic relations.

The Peking summit, in addition, was a diplomatic and political exercise in opposites, and its working procedures were unique.

On the one hand, the business sessions were conducted in total secrecy. No information—not even the subjects being discussed—was announced or "leaked" to the press until after the joint communiqué was issued in Shanghai at the end of a week of negotiations. Even then, only the bare bones of the vigorously debated issues that divide the two countries were disclosed. The minutes of the meetings between the American and Chinese officials at various levels are the most important top secret documents in existence today.

On the other hand, President Nixon and Chinese Premier Chou En-lai were costarred in a week-long, live and living color television extravaganza—a production of electronic age "circuses" for the public watching as an earlier public watched the great spectaculars produced by the Roman emperors.

Nixon and Chou planned both of these parallel and opposite approaches to the Peking summit. They collaborated in engaging in the deepest secret diplomacy since World War II. They also collaborated in putting on an extraordinary public show.

All in all, Nixon spent fifteen hours in formal business meetings with the Chinese leaders—one hour with Chairman Mao Tse-tung on the day of his arrival on February 21 and more than fourteen working hours at formal meetings with Premier Chou. In addition, Nixon spent more than twenty-four hours in the company of Chou at social events and informal discussions.

But the real work of the summit conference was done by two men who are the most respected advisers and confidants of Nixon and Chou—Dr. Henry A. Kissinger, the President's chief National Security Adviser, whose first secret mission to Peking last July made this conference possible, and Chiao Kuan-hua, China's Deputy Foreign Minister, Chou's right-hand man in foreign affairs, and the man who led Peking's first delegation to the United Nations General Assembly in New York last fall.

Kissinger and Chiao, rather than the foreign ministers of China and the United States, were the real diplomats of this conference. They spent countless hours together during the negotiating process and, finally, in hammering out a joint communiqué.

Neither Secretary of State Rogers nor Chinese Foreign Minister Chi, for example, attended the four major bargaining sessions between Nixon and Chou. They attended only the other two plenary sessions, which were procedural and pro forma.

Nixon was accompanied at the important meetings with Chou only by Kissinger, John Holdridge, a China specialist on Kissinger's staff, and Winston Lord, Kissinger's "man Friday" in the National Security Council. No one from the State Department—not even Rogers—was present.

The Chinese side of the important Nixon-Chou meetings was equally restricted. In addition to Chiao (Kissinger's opposite number), there was Marshal Yeh Chien-ying, who seems to have taken over many of the functions of the purged Defense Minister, Lin Piao; and the deputy director of the Foreign Ministry's protocol section, Wang Hai-june, Chairman Mao's niece, who also was a principal assistant to Chiao at the United Nations last fall.

The only available information about how the summit conference worked has come from Kissinger, who held an extraordinary press conference in Shanghai after the communiqué was issued—a press conference attended by Chinese and American press as well as Third World news people. The Chinese held no press conference. Chou said at the airport after Nixon departed that the communiqué—in which China won many points—"speaks for itself."

Kissinger volunteered this version of the procedure of the summit meeting:

The procedure that was followed here was that issues of general principle were first discussed in the meetings between the President and the Prime Minister. They were then, after they had been explored for some time, transferred to the meetings chaired by the Secretary of State [Rogers] and the Foreign Minister of the People's Republic of China [Chi]. Then, if any additional issues arose, they might be referred back to the meeting of the President and the Prime Minister. [Although Chou usually is referred to as Premier, Nixon and Kissinger refer to him as the Prime Minister.]

In drafting the communiqué, various sections were produced by various elements of the American side. I played the role of go-between on our side and the Vice Foreign Minister [Chiao], whose name I despair of ever learning to pronounce, on the Chinese side.

In this manner, as we put together the various paragraphs that were supplied to us on our side by various individuals, if we reached a point at which agreement seemed near or possible, we would then go back to our principals and to the Secretary of State. Through this process, the communiqué was finally achieved.

For example, some of the sessions were quite prolonged. The last few nights the sessions [between Kissinger and Chiao] went on until the early hours of the morning. . . . In Peking, the Chinese delegation had a house in the guest complex [near Nixon's villa], and most of the sessions took place in that house. As a paragraph [of the communiqué] was finished, it would typically go back to the President who was in the next house, and this went on Friday night [February 25] until about 5:30 in the morning."

President Nixon assembled the American press corps at his villa in Hangchow late Saturday (February 26) afternoon, ostensibly to let them see the lavish villa he was occupying and to pose with the news people for a group picture.

Because there were no diplomatic relations with China, Nixon said, the talks had to be held in absolute secrecy:

Getting here was a long road and it had to be handled with very great discretion. It was a long road also for them [the Chinese]. . . .

Once we were here, the talks had to be held in an atmosphere quite different from those where we already have diplomatic relations. I can only say that whatever we have achieved—and you will have to judge that—would have been seriously jeopardized, and possibly not achieved at all, if at any time we had yielded to the pressure of the press for news. The inevitable result might have been—well—it would have jeopardized whatever we did accomplish. . . .

I believe in this instance you [the press] have served perhaps a higher interest of nurturing this new relationship with China, which was so delicate and so easily could have been ruptured.

Following is the list of the official meetings Nixon had with leaders of the People's Republic of China:

Monday, February 21—Meeting with Chairman Mao Tsetung at Mao's residence. Only Kissinger accompanied Nixon. Length of meeting—one hour.

Monday, February 21—Plenary meeting of all American and Chinese delegates with Nixon and Chou in the Great Hall of the People—one hour.

Tuesday, February 22—Restricted meeting between Nixon and Chou—three hours and fifty minutes.

Wednesday, February 23—Restricted meeting between Nixon and Chou—four hours.

Thursday, February 24—Restricted meeting between Nixon and Chou at Nixon's guest house—three hours. (Chou also stayed for dinner and continued informal conversations for another three hours.)

Friday, February 25—Restricted meeting between Nixon and Chou—one hour.

Saturday, February 26—Plenary meeting at Peking airport before leaving for Hangchow—one hour.

There were, of course, many other occasions for informal talks. The final one took place the morning Nixon left

Shanghai to return to Washington, Monday, February 28, when Nixon and Chou talked for one hour—after the communiqué was issued.

CEREMONIALS

BY BOB CONSIDINE

A venerable and venerated Chinese Proverb (pre-Mao, but still accepted in the People's Republic of China) states that a journey of a thousand miles begins with a single step.

In the case of President Nixon, his Journey for Peace, which all but equaled the mileage of the circumference of the earth, began with a single banquet. Three more glittering demonstrations of Chinese gastronomy awaited him, Mrs. Nixon, his elite corps, and those of us who tagged along. But the first one was an event of many ramifications. The President's welcoming committee at the airport, headed by Premier Chou En-lai, was as correctly frozen as a group from Madame Tussaud's.

Hence, it was a relief to all concerned when the Premier hosted the first of the visit's banquets. It opened wide the Bamboo Curtain, whose parting had been so reluctant and seemingly begrudging. Suddenly, the more or less mortal enemies of the past twenty-three years were clicking tiny glasses of an insecure little red wine and an outrageously explosive sorghum-based "white mule."

There was no head table, as such, American-style. The principal people sat at a large table on the same floor as the many other guests. The hors d'oeuvres were as endless as the Great Wall of China. These lesser dishes surrounded a succession of great dishes: spongy bamboo shoots and egg-white consommé, shark's fin in three shreds, fried and stewed prawns, mushrooms and mustard greens, steamed chicken with coconut, almond junket (soup), pastries and fruit—laced throughout by good Chinese *pei jou* (beer) and the aforementioned spirits.

Somewhere during the scheduled consumption of food, burning-black-eyed Chou En-lai, a trim seventy-three-year-old man-of-the-world in his well-tailored "Mao suit," went up to the plain stage above the banquet floor and proposed a toast in Mandarin.

Upon the conclusion of his toast remarks, the man who oversees the daily operations domestically and internationally of about 800 million human beings moved in easy cadence to the President and his party, to touch glasses and take a conservative sip, and then along to all the tables of the first row in the massive hall.

Plainly emboldened, the President stepped to the mike of the stage decorated by the flags of the U.S. and the P.R.C. to make his toast.

The next evening, the President and his suite were exposed to (and found themselves applauding) the ballet form of the most persuasive propaganda pitch in China, the *Red Detachment of Women.*

The following day, he and his group, ensconced in impressive, black, Chinese-built limousines, shot up to the Great Wall to interview Barbara Walters, Harry Reasoner, and Eric Sevareid.

The President and his lady figuratively poked chopsticks into the delicate texture of mysterious Chinese hospitality, and extracted bits that nourished not only themselves but appreciative hosts.

Ever since Sheba's visit to Solomon, it has been a custom to exchange gifts when heads of state meet. President Nixon presented Chou En-lai with a handsome leather-bound album of American scenic wonders. Later, he sent two musk oxen from the San Francisco Zoo, a 300-pound cow and her 100-pound brother.

Much accord was reached over the ceremony of drinking tea together, the mutual thrill of the final night's acrobatic show, the whispered confidences at the ballet, the communion of applause when a cyclist carried thirteen fellow artists around the stage.

All this folderol was not really folderol at all. It was the mortar that secured and bound the masonry of an accord that conceivably could last decades or centuries beyond the principals themselves.

WITH THE FIRST LADY

BY HELEN THOMAS

America's First Lady is at home anywhere in the world. She relates to people. That is where she shines, more so than any other President's wife in recent history.

China was a historic first for Pat Nixon—the seventy-fifth foreign country she has toured as the wife of a public figure. "People are the same the world over," she reminisced on the homeward-bound flight aboard *The Spirit of '76* after the week-long journey for peace. "I think they're good people, and it all depends on the leadership," she observed.

As she does for every trip Mrs. Nixon did her homework—in depth, perhaps more so for the Peking pilgrimage because she knew its epic dimensions in terms of international diplomacy and peace in the Pacific.

In that respect she was in the company of the New Left in the U.S. She had read her little red book of Mao's *Quotations,* so that when the friendly female political commissars brought up the "thoughts" of China's godlike ruler, Mrs. Nixon was well versed and knew what to expect.

Without getting into a debate on the touchy subject of democracy and capitalism versus socialism, Mrs. Nixon simply would say, "Oh yes, I am acquainted with his philosophy."

Despite the all-pervading atmosphere of Maoism, the First Lady managed to avoid dialectical discussions with her Chinese hostesses, most of whom were the top women in the ranks of the Revolutionary Committees.

Mrs. Nixon was not rubbing shoulders with Communists for the first time. As a veteran globetrotter, she has visited four Communist countries behind the Iron Curtain: the Soviet Union, Poland, Roumania, and Yugoslavia.

The President's wife, who celebrates her sixtieth birthday on March 16, has never looked more lovely—regal in her clothes and exuding warmth and understanding in her manner. She personified good taste, bringing along eight elegant but simple dresses created by her favorite New York designers. They were a striking contrast to the drab blue and gray pants suits worn by her Communist counterparts. Mrs. Nixon also brought along her "longies" and boots for the bitter wintry weather.

She wore only pearl earrings during the day and a diamond brooch on her shoulder at night. The Chinese women wore no makeup and no jewelry, except for a red and gold Mao button, which added a touch of color to their stark appearance. There appeared to be no expression of envy or resentment on the part of the Chinese ladies who once wore the sexiest gowns ever created, with their high slits up the sides of their tight-fitting sheaths and their Mandarin collars.

Just as Mrs. Nixon was interested in their life-styles, as they became more acquainted, the Chinese women began to ask questions about her life, the White House, the role of American women, and her daughters, Tricia Cox and Julie Eisenhower.

Known for her boundless energy, Mrs. Nixon found herself programed throughout the trip, and her hosts were well briefed on her life, her likes, and her dislikes. But her pace was much less frenetic than past trips and there were many more tea breaks and rest stops than she has experienced in her wide travels.

With a pied piper entourage of reporters and cameramen, including the top stars of network television, Mrs. Nixon made her rounds, traveling in an impressive "Red Flag" black-curtained limousine. She went to the Evergreen People's Commune, a short distance outside Peking, and told the smiling Revolutionary Committee members and the awed peasants that she had been raised on a farm in California. She dropped in on a clinic and—with some hesitation, at first—watched two young girls perform acupuncture on a frail, elderly woman, turning her into a human pincushion. She found she could bear to witness the ancient Chinese method of anesthesia by applying long gold and silver needles into nerve centers because "It didn't seem to pain the patient." She also was pleased to note the needles did not leave scars.

She dropped in on a classroom where she was enchanted with the rosy-cheeked, pigtailed children, wearing bright-colored blouses over long pants, who sang, with all their hearts. "We are going to Tienanmen Square to see Chairman Mao." Overhead was the Mao calligraphy "Serve the People."

She carried the ball pictorially. She gave cameramen a field day when she displayed her skill in the use of chopsticks, while touring the Peking Hotel to study the art of Chinese cookery.

At the Summer Palace in Peking, she strolled through the Gate of Longevity and Goodwill. "That's prophetic," she laughed. She admired the jade, gold, and cloisonné—priceless relics of the past, and even the heavy scent of incense.

At the Peking Children's Hospital she donned a long, white physician's smock and hugged the youngsters with affection. And at the Children's Palace, she found much evidence of her own pet project—volunteerism.

Some of her major sightseeing was done in the company of her husband. At the sixteenth-century Ming Tombs, she marveled at the richness of the Oriental past. In the Forbidden City, she walked in the snow, wearing a mink coat, uncaring that snowflakes would muss her hairdo. The complex of palaces with pagoda-like roofs was a reminder of China's great architecture, which she much preferred to the grim, mammoth structures of the post-Liberation days, which were heavily influenced by the Soviets.

Every evening she attended a banquet, most involving twelve courses of Chinese delicacies. During the day she would limit her intake to green tea and tangerines, in order to face the epicurean fare the Chinese served in the evening.

She met the famous Chiang Ching, Mao's wife, only once. They sat together at the *Red Detachment of Women,* a ballet extolling the peasant revolt against oppressive landlords. She met Premier Chou En-lai's wife twice, first at the guest house on the day of her arrival, again at the ballet.

Mrs. Nixon saw more of Chou, who sat beside her at the sumptuous dinners, speaking in English because she teased him into it. "He's a charmer," said Mrs. Nixon. "He's a man who knows the world. He has a delightful sense of humor."

Like any woman would, Mrs. Nixon had to see the shops

of Peking. She picked up a pair of off-white silk pajamas with green piping "for Dick," a dozen cups and saucers in the white and blue rice pattern, and gold silk brocade for Tricia. "I couldn't go back without gifts for the girls," she said gaily.

While she spread goodwill among her new friends, she surveyed the scene personally, forming her own judgments on the merits of the socialistic system under Chairman Mao. But she made no public pronouncements, knowing that she could upset the applecart at a delicate moment in history. "If I make comments, I might spoil it," she said. "I like to point out the things which the country is proud of." She did tell an interviewer she thought Chinese children were getting a "well-rounded education."

She was astounded at the amount of time she spent talking to her Chinese hostesses about the preparation of food. Although she enjoys Oriental cuisine, she did not bring home any cookbooks for the White House chef to try.

In many ways, she was the eyes and ears for her husband during her stay on the mainland. She met the people and talked to them, while he was locked in a serious dialogue with Chou and, on one occasion, with Mao.

During their sightseeing jaunts together, Mrs. Nixon always let the President take center stage, walking behind, keeping out of the camera's view. Frequently the President would beckon to her to join him up front on the tours, but as she put it, "I wasn't the main event." Nor was there any desire on her part to steal the show, although she did at times, because she was doing the warm, human things. "I bring you greetings from the American children," she would say to the bright, smiling, well-fed Chinese girls and boys who knew that she had come to visit from far-off America.

So colorful were her tours, she had author James Michener trailing her for *Reader's Digest* most of the time. Conservative columnist William Buckley also realized that hers was the only show in town, and covered Mrs. Nixon at the Children's Palace. When a classroom of young musicians played "Billy Boy," Buckley grinned and said, "They're playing my song."

When Chou paused in front of a cage of lovebirds at a charming park on West Lake in Hangchow, and the birds began embracing with their necks and beaks, the Premier giggled and looked at Mrs. Nixon in a slightly flustered way. She smoothed over the situation. "Lovey dovey," she trilled. As they moved to another cage, Chou said something in Chinese to the birds. "I talk to my bird like that, too," Mrs. Nixon said.

She passed around an LBJ-style invitation to the tune of "Y'all come" to her Chinese friends. And it was sincere. She hopes their trip will spur more return visits on the part of the Chinese. "I hope they will come," she said, in a gesture to further open the door to China-U.S. relations.

Speaking of the Chinese, she observed, "They have a long history of being gracious and talented people. I'm so happy they haven't lost it." She noted with pleasure that Chinese women were taking an active part in their government and had major roles on the Revolutionary Committees. "I feel they have made great progress," she said.

"It's a wonderful memory," said the First Lady. "I have never met more friendly or considerate people."

HANGCHOW

BY STAN CARTER

Hangchow, the second city that President and Mrs. Nixon visited, is the storybook China of pagodas, lotus blossoms, tea, and silk that we all imagined in our youth.

Marco Polo, who visited the resort at the end of the thirteenth century, called it "the greatest city which may be found in the world, where so many pleasures may be found that one fancies himself to be in paradise."

Built between wooded hillsides and a velvet-smooth lake ringed with weeping willows and peach trees, Hangchow was a really swinging town in the Italian explorer's time. There were countless restaurants, taverns, brothels, and theaters, along with strolling musicians, jugglers, storytellers, and performing animals. Fleets of pleasure boats nudged through a floating carpet of lotus leaves on the Shi Hu, an irregularly-shaped body of water about two leagues around. Its name in English is West Lake.

Hangchow is a quieter place now. There are still tea houses scattered around town, but they are not the gathering places that they used to be, where people spent entire afternoons gossiping and playing mah jongg. But it is still a beautiful city, with a generally mild climate, and many Chinese from Shanghai, Canton, and other parts of the country still go there on holidays. Along with fishing boats, there is still a flotilla of scow-shaped, motor-powered tourist boats on the lake.

Chairman Mao Tse-tung, who likes to get away from the cold winters in Peking, spends much time in Hangchow. Local officials insist that they are "not quite clear" about what the founder of the Chinese People's Republic does, or where he stays during his visits. But it is obvious from the furnishings that he resides at least part of the time in the same government guest house where the Nixons were put up during their twenty-hour visit.

The guest house is a pale green stucco building with a red-tiled, pagoda-style roof, in a secluded, easily guarded complex of pagodas, pavilions, gazebos, and carefully tended formal gardens just outside of town. There is only one access road. There are several ponds on one side and West Lake on the other. The guest house was built in 1959, during Mao's ill-fated Great Leap Forward, when China tried to accomplish ten years of expansion in one year.

Although no one in the American party counted them, it was estimated that the house had at least thirty rooms. The toilets were covered with silk padding.

Even for February, it was unusually chilly in Hangchow during the Nixons' visit, about thirty degrees Fahrenheit, and the skies were gray. The lawns in the guest house gardens, which must be plushy soft and green in the spring, were brown and dead looking. But a solitary peach tree was in pink bloom and willows hung wistfully over the ponds.

Accompanied by Premier Chou, the President and his party flew to Hangchow from Peking in two Soviet-built,

Chinese-owned Ilyushin-18 turboprop airliners. The Chairman and all the members of the Chekiang Province Revolutionary Committee met them, applauding as Nixon walked down the red-carpeted ramp from the plane, followed by Chou, and then by Mrs. Nixon. In the Chinese custom, Nixon applauded back.

Nixon had stayed up in Peking until 5 A.M. that day working on the communiqué summing up his talks with Chou and Mao. Nevertheless, he appeared in an ebullient mood and did not look tired. Chatting with me later in the day, the President explained, "Some people wear out inside and some outside. I wear out inside."

During the afternoon, Chou took Nixon and his wife on a one-and-a-half hour boat ride on West Lake. They walked through the Park of the Orioles Singing in the Willows on their way to the boat dock, and Chou pointed out where a redwood seedling—one of the gifts that the President had brought from the United States—had been planted. It was on a small, grassy slope, near a camelia bush, a pine, and several other trees.

The Premier said this had been the wrong place to put the foot-high seedling, because it eventually would grow very large.

"The Prime Minister pays attention to everything," Nixon commented.

Later they came to a large meadow and Chou said the redwood should have been planted there.

"It takes so long to grow," Nixon answered.

"The next generations can enjoy it," the Premier said.

The Nixons threw fish food to goldfish at the edge of the lake. There weren't many because of the cold weather, which kept most of the fish at the bottom of the lake. But Nixon marveled at the size of those he saw, more than one foot long. Mrs. Nixon gave an empty fish food package to an interpreter and asked him to put it in his pocket because "I don't want to get arrested for littering."

They rode in a wooden motorboat with a large, enclosed cabin to the largest of four islands on the lake, called Three

(continued on page 129)

The President's Trip to China

3

4

1 On the steps of *Spirit of '76,* just before departure from Andrews Air Force Base.

2 On board the President's plane en route to China: Henry A. Kissinger and the President.

3 The Nixons prepare for their visit.

4 From left, Assistant Secretary of State Marshall Green, Dr. Kissinger, the President, and Secretary of State William P. Rogers.

5 Arrival at Capital Airport, Peking.

6 A 500-man Chinese military honor guard awaits the
7 arrival of the presidential party.

8 Premier Chou En-lai welcomes the President,
9 with a historic handshake at Peking Airport.

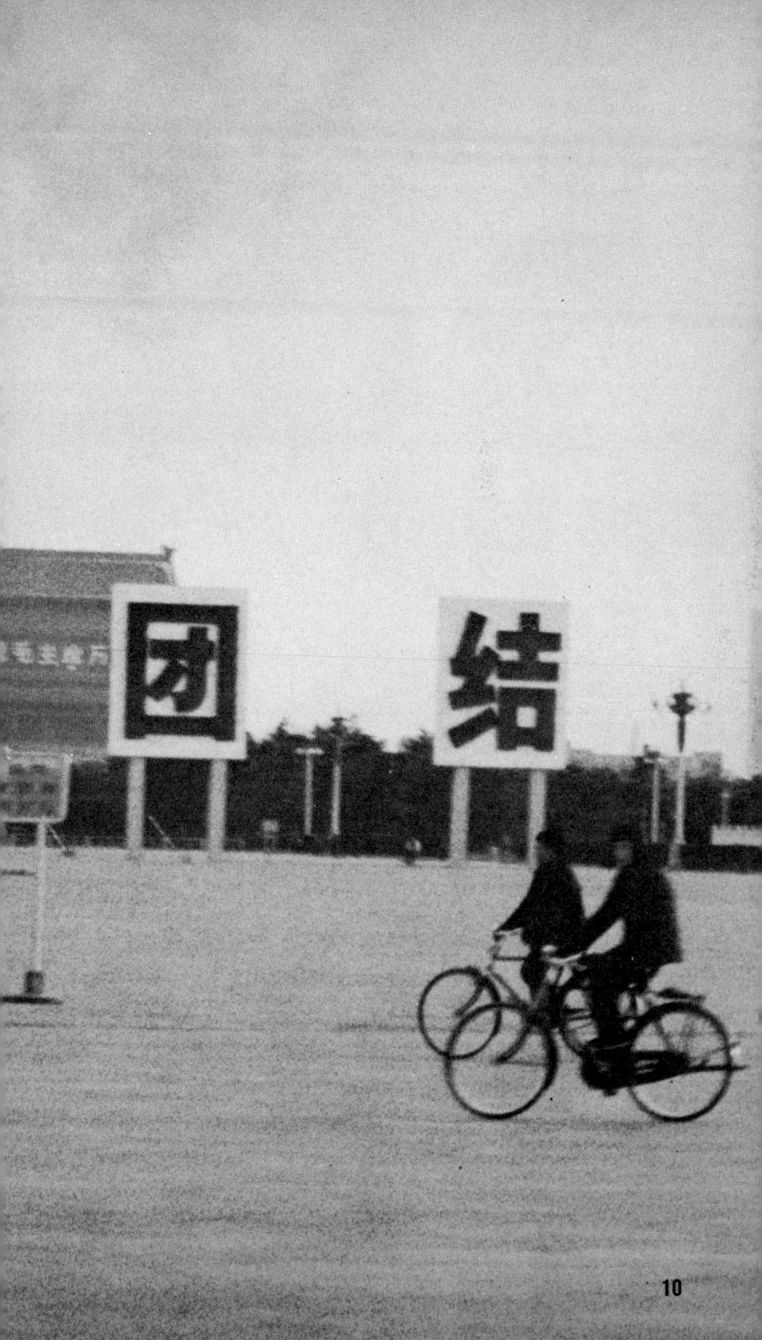
团
结

12

13

15

16

19

20

The President meets
Chairman Mao Tse-tung.

On the next two pages, left
to right, Chou, interpreter
Tang Wen-sheng, Mao,
Nixon; Kissinger
was on Nixon's left.

26

28

36

37

艰苦奋斗
勤俭建国

54

全世界人民大团结万岁！

LONG LIVE THE GREAT UNITY OF THE PEOPLE OF THE WORLD!

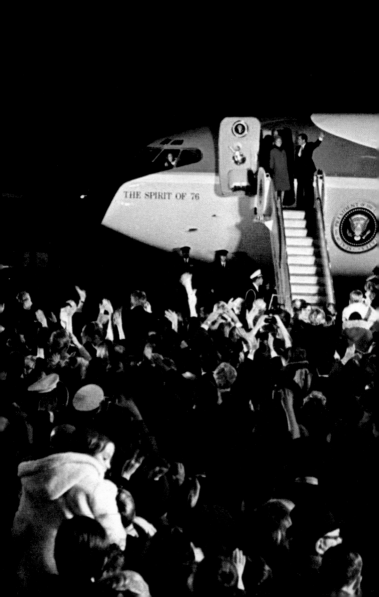

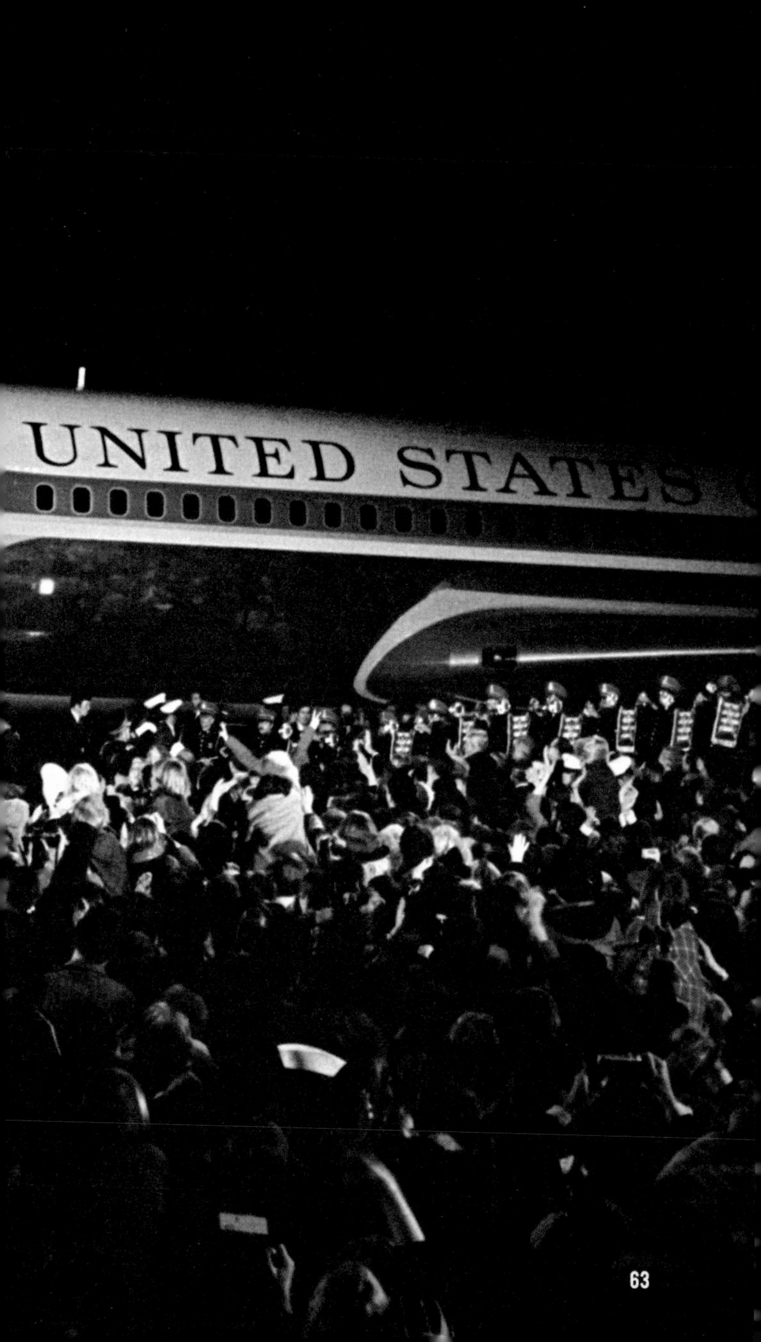
UNITED STATES

60 Views of West Lake, Hangchow.
61

62 President and Premier bid farewell, Shanghai.

63 President and Mrs. Nixon are
64 welcomed home at Andrews Air Force Base.

(continued from page 33)

Pools That Mirror the Moon, and walked around the island, stopping to inspect two summer buildings with green tile roofs.

Turning toward the mainland, Nixon commented, "It looks like a postcard with those mountains in the background."

A couple of minutes later, he asked the Premier, "Chairman Mao likes this place very much, doesn't he?"

Chou nodded yes.

On Saturday night, the provincial Revolutionary Committee gave a banquet for the Nixons. The food was southern style, different than they had been having in Peking—cold dishes in eight small plates, Hangchow roast chicken, West Lake fish in sweet and sour sauce, shrimps with green tea leaves, fried duck with spices, fried chicken squares with onions and peanuts, bamboo shoots stewed in peanut oil, ham soup with scallops, chrysanthemum cakes, egg rolls with sugar and sesame fillings, lotus seeds in rock sugar, and fruit. The lotus seeds tasted like roasted chestnuts. Nan Ping, Chairman of the provincial Revolutionary Committee, thanked Nixon for the gift of redwood tree seedlings and said, "We hope that they will continuously grow taller and stronger as a symbol of the friendship between the Chinese and American people."

"Now that we have been here, now that we have seen the splendor of this city, we realize why it has been said that heaven is above and beneath are Hangchow and Soochow," Nixon said. "I am sure that the proud citizens of this province would say that Peking is the head of China, but Hangchow is the heart of China."

SHANGHAI

BY ROBERT L. KEATLEY

Seventy years ago, an American missionary found Shanghai a bustling port which "displays to the Chinese the marvels of Western skill, knowledge, and enterprise." He also found it a city where foreign settlers, cloistered in their concession areas taken from resentful Chinese, practiced "justice and humanity" as an object lesson for the natives.

The late Edgar Snow brought a keener eye a few decades later. His Shanghai featured "glitter and glamour; pompous wealth beside naked starvation . . . with well-dressed Chinese in their chauffeured limousines behind bulletproof glass . . . [plus] generations of foreign families who call Shanghai home and live quiet conservative lives in their tiny vacuums untouched by China." Sin city it was then, with "sailors in their smelly bars and friendly brothels on Szechuan Road; the myriad short-term whores and pimps busily darting in and out of alleyways"—all adding up to "the vast slum that was Shanghai."

Neither place is the Shanghai that Richard Nixon visited in 1972. Long gone are the rapacious capitalism, the foreign quarters, and red-light districts that made China's largest city so infamous years ago. During his brief stopovers (the President both entered and departed China via that port), Mr. Nixon got a brief look at what is now an austere manufacturing and trading center, one which may soon see American ships sailing up the Whangpoo River, thanks to trade agreements expected from the presidential trip.

The city now conforms to the unique socialist teachings of Chairman Mao Tse-tung—it is in fact home to China's more leftist political leadership—yet it somehow retains reminders of its wheeling and dealing past. This lingers despite the abolition of private businesses, the turning of suburbs into People's Communes and the eradication of the garish night life—so contrary to the puritanical mores of Chinese-style communism—which seems gone forever.

But Shanghai today is still one of China's most fascinating cities. Alone of major population centers it boasts a Western-style skyline, the old Bund or waterfront business district. It also has a distinct commercial center where crowded shops swarm with customers daily (Shanghai work schedules are staggered as factories rotate the weekly day off to equalize strains on transport and utilities; "Some people get their Sunday on Wednesday," a resident noted).

The stores along Nanking Road, still the main drag as in

pre-Communist days, feature a wider variety of goods than the popular blue ant image of China would suggest. Colorful fabrics (more often for children's clothes than for their parents), fresh foods, the varied household pots and pans essential for Chinese cuisine, are among them. The Shanghai No. 1 Department Store, in fact, boasts 27,000 different products and 100,000 buyers daily—200,000 at holiday time. A visitor finds thirty-three different sizes, shapes, and colors of toothbrushes on sale, for example, and even (for some reason) baseballs in the sports department.

Traces of the old days linger elsewhere. Along the Bund, early every morning, teachers instruct children in the ritual sword dances of the Peking Opera, or in acrobatics. Old folks cluster in the small park opposite the former British Consulate (the one that once allegedly forbade "Chinese and dogs"); for three Chinese cents' admission, they find a quiet waterfront spot for practicing Tai Chai-chuan, the ancient exercise the West inaccurately calls "Chinese shadowboxing." On warm evenings, it's even possible to find courting couples holding hands on park benches—a public display of affection seldom seen elsewhere in Mao's China.

Unfortunately, the President didn't see much of this; his visit lasted only twenty-four hours and much was devoted to either political summitry or needed rest after a grueling week of negotiations and ritual sightseeing. Yet he apparently sensed enough of this lively (by modern Chinese standards) place to praise in a banquet toast "the vibrancy of a great city, Shanghai."

However, the Nixons did get a glimpse of industrial achievements, which are a source of pride to many Chinese who formerly saw economic assets controlled by foreigners and a rich minority. "Shanghai has become a comprehensive industrial base" for the entire nation, the official New China News Agency boasted shortly before the presidential arrival.

The Nixons' closest look came at the vast Shanghai Industrial Exhibition, which local officials consider a must stop for all visitors. It's a more than 10,000-square-yard display case of local products, an ornate structure built in the Stalinist style emulated so often when Russians were close friends. President Nixon spent ninety minutes touring the exhibit, seemingly interested though confessing he didn't understand machinery well, when confronted with complex gear, that whirled and clanked for their own unique purposes.

He began in the main hall, featuring machines for generating electricity, cutting metal, and forging shapes, among others. "Machinery has always impressed me," the President told his hosts, including Premier Chou En-lai, "and I know nothing about it. All I can do is change a tire on a car." Looking at something called a spiral bevel generator, Mr. Nixon started to push a button but was stopped by an attendent. "He knows I don't know how to operate it," the Chief Executive conceded.

Later, though, he did push another machine's main button, and the device dutifully coughed up a small gear.

Consummate politician that he is, Mr. Nixon may have been more interested in the show's assorted political implications than in its industrial accomplishments, which no casual visitor can evaluate accurately. For one thing, the building used to be called the Sino-Soviet People's Friendship Hall, a name attached to many buildings throughout China which now operate under different titles. The split between the two Communist giants, of course, does much to explain why any American President could be in Shanghai in the first place.

In addition to complex machines, the hall also exhibited remaining traces of the Mao cult which the Chairman himself ordered toned down a year or so ago. Outside the main entrance stood a thirty-foot gilded statue of the venerable Communist Party chieftain who helped found the party fifty-one years ago in Shanghai. Inside there was more. At the far end of the main room, a white plaster statue of the Chairman—outstretched arm pointing to a brighter future—looked down upon the touring American leader. Throughout, signs noted the chairman's assorted thoughts had helped create the industrial wonders on display.

And there was a little live-action politicking as well. President and Premier engaged in wide-ranging repartee for the benefit of TV cameras filming their tour. For example, Mr. Nixon delivered a little lecture to his hosts: "Competition should always be friendly; it is not necessary to be antagonistic; each can do his best." To which one Chinese replied, "Sometimes in the past people have competed in antagonism."

Mr. Chou also took the opportunity to stress how technology has advanced under Communist leadership. He noted that several girl workers on hand were granddaughters of illiterate peasants. Always charming to the ladies, the Premier also said that women can usually do any technical job that men normally handle, a view that may not be completely shared by his presidential guest—something of a traditionalist in such matters.

Mr. Nixon was probably aware also of some other political facts during his Shanghai stopover. The city was birthplace of the Cultural Revolution, the political movement inspired by Chairman Mao that disrupted much urban life in the late sixties. Even today—despite public evidence of relaxation—its leadership remains in the vanguard of China's political left wing.

The experts contend that if any segment of the leadership opposed the Nixon visit, this was it. It may have been no accident that Shanghai's top two leaders didn't appear at the airport when Mr. Nixon made a refueling stop en route to Peking. Although the ranking men did greet the President when he returned for his official stay, the number two—the ruling Politburo's youngest leader and a renowned ideologue—never did appear, in either Shanghai or Peking. It will take time to know positively, but it's possible these men pressured Premier Chou in an effort to avoid having him become too chummy with the Western leader, once denounced as a warmonger "who will never become a Buddha," and seek peace.

In fact, the top man, Chang Chun-chiao, expressed this concern in a guarded way at the banquet he hosted on Mr. Nixon's last night in China. Shanghai people are "keeping the initiative in our own hands and relying on our own efforts," he said pointedly, a reference to the Maoist principle of never becoming dependent on foreign powers (as, to its eventual sorrow, China once depended on the Soviet Union). Memories of past exploitation are particularly bitter in Shanghai, and close relations with any outsiders are still viewed with suspicion by the leadership there—though the general public seems less uptight.

Mr. Nixon didn't let this pass unnoticed. In his response, he noted Mr. Chang's merely pro forma reference to mutual friendship and proposed his own toast "to that friendship between our two peoples to which Chairman Chang has referred so eloquently"—thus neatly slipping him a share of responsibility for the incongruous appearance of an American President in a Maoist stronghold.

Afterward a tired President—perhaps feeling both the strain of a hard week's work and the *mao-tai* liquor consumed during toasts—drowsed through a "soiree" featuring acrobatics: Acts including traditional Chinese conjuring, trick cycling, and a slapstick comedy skit performed by inept cooks. Though it struck many Americans as early Ed Sullivan at best, the indefatigable Premier Chou seemed to enjoy it. After the magician pulled two lambs from his cape, the Premier explained that new ones had to be recruited regularly because they always outgrew their jobs.

The Shanghai stay ended early Monday—a brief stopover from which such items as a visit to the Bund had to be omitted from the presidential schedule. After a rare (for this trip) good night's sleep, Mr. Nixon met Premier Chou for an hour, then motored to the airport for liftoff from Chinese soil. Along the way, he drew the largest crowds seen in China, for in most places the general public was kept at a distance; Shanghai people along the streets seemed politely curious but reserved.

For many Americans, the relative bustle and variety of Shanghai upgraded their image of China (as the clever Premier Chou reportedly expected), and they responded affirmatively when he told the departing visitors, "I wish you would all come back again."

THE RESPONSE OF THE CHINESE PEOPLE

BY ROBERT S. BOYD

Despite a generation of isolation and angry propaganda, the first American "army" to appear on the mainland of China since 1948 found itself in friendly territory. The more than 300 U.S. officials, technicians, and correspondents who accompanied the President and Mrs. Nixon were regarded with indifference, mild curiosity, or some amusement by the Chinese man in the street. We were the targets of enormous, at times excessive, politeness and helpfulness by the middle- and low-level officials assigned to our care and feeding. And at the summit level, the President's reception by Chairman Mao Tse-tung and Premier Chou En-lai was remarkably cordial in view of past animosities and the deep difference on matters of substance between them.

An occasional minor incident ruffled the surface harmony. Shortly before the President arrived, two members of the advance party fell sick and had to be sent home. The Peking correspondent for Reuters, James Pringle, heard about it and filed a brief report. His story was noted by Chinese officials, who erroneously assumed the Americans had violated the ban on leaking news before Nixon came. To punish the miscreant technicians, the Chinese for two days took away the bowls of candy in their working quarters. The Americans were quite indignant at the loss of their candy.

There were times, though, when our antics delighted the Chinese. An NBC associate producer, Fred Flamenhaft, was among a group of Americans invited by some Chinese to dine at the justly famed Peking Roast Duck Restaurant one evening. There were many toasts in fiery *mao-tai* brandy to blend generalities like "peace" and "friendship." Flamenhaft was well primed with *mao-tai* when his turn came to propose a toast. He loudly declared, "I don't give a damn what you all said, I've just had the best meal of my life, and I toast the duck!" The Chinese hosts broke up laughing.

Sometimes the Chinese efforts to be helpful went too far. In preparation for the Americans' visit, the toilet seats in our hotel in Peking were refinished. A sumac extract in the lacquer caused poison-ivy-like boils on the bottoms of 23 American advance men and seven Chinese interpreters brought in from the provinces for the occasion. The U.S. Public Health Service in Washington finally diagnosed the problem and word was passed to beware of the seats.

Chinese reactions to the American invasion depended on the rank and status of the Chinese. They broke down into four groups:

1. At the very top, Chairman Mao broke precedent by receiving Nixon at his home only three and a half hours after the President reached Peking, and by permitting Chinese television to film the scene. After Mao had given his benediction to the trip, the muted initial official reaction suddenly blossomed into effusive cordiality and a publicity binge in the controlled Chinese press. For that week, there was almost a "Cult of Chairman Nixon," as his name and picture appeared day after day on the front page of *People's Daily*.

2. At a lower level, the Foreign Ministry officials, guides, and interpreters who were supposed to help us were kind and generally efficient, but at times they seemed frustrated by the disorderly work style of the American press. When my baggage was lost for twenty-four hours, my escort seemed genuinely distressed, and fell back on Chairman Mao's thought: "We still have many shortcomings in our work. We must think hard and try to do better."

Some of our nannies fussed or balked at the whims of U.S. correspondents, who kept wanting to change the program the Chinese had painstakingly worked out for us. At times, when questions got too embarrassing, they simply clammed up. At lunch one day, columnist Joseph Kraft asked an official in Shanghai about Lin Piao, the former Defense Minister who was purged last September. "Eat your lunch," the official replied.

Criticism did not always go down too well. Appearing on a Today Show broadcast from Peking, columnist William Buckley lambasted the radical surgery performed on Peking

University during the Great Proletarian Cultural Revolution. A Chinese interpreter, who had been with Buckley during his visit to the university, reacted as if he had been kicked in the stomach and refused to speak to Buckley afterward.

3. A third set of reactions was observed among the "ordinary citizens" who were preprogramed by the Chinese to come into contact with Americans. These were the factory workers, agricultural commune members, school teachers, and students, and the like on the official tour list for the President or Mrs. Nixon and the press. They were invariably exceedingly polite and friendly. We were always introduced as "American friends." They would beam and clap whenever we entered a room. Even doctors and patients in a hospital operating theater paused in order to applaud us.

Most Chinese whom we encountered turned away when we tried to photograph them. Exceptions were the groups of well-dressed, happy Chinese who had obviously been pre-positioned at the Great Wall, in the Ming Tombs, and in the lakeside park at Hangchow to provide a pleasant picture for the presidential party. They posed willingly for the cameras.

4. Finally, the reaction of the real "ordinary Chinese" was, of course, impossible for an outsider to determine with only eight days in China and a few scraps of the language. The inner thoughts of the stony-faced young People's Liberation Army soldiers who guarded our hotels, or the impassive waiters, elevator operators, and shop clerks who served us are a mystery. In one sense, perhaps, it doesn't really matter very much what they thought. There is no "public opinion" in the American sense in China. People are told what to think.

Three Chinese of widely varying location and rank gave almost the same response when asked what they thought of the Nixon visit. The vice commander of the 196th People's Liberation Army division based sixty miles southeast of Peking, a member of a commune ten miles south of the capital, and a factory worker touring the Ming Tombs, north of the city, all said, in effect: Your president asked to come to our country; Chairman Mao said it was all right for him to come; so we welcome him.

This passive, unexcited Chinese response to what we Americans considered a sensational event was mirrored by the visible behavior of the people in the streets and shops. If they happened to be lined up at a bus stop or walking along the sidewalk when the President came by, they would gaze curiously, but they rarely waved or smiled. They were not told when or where Nixon would appear next, so they could not make an effort to go out to see him, even if they had wanted to.

When the President and Mrs. Nixon visited the Ming Tombs, some Chinese tourists gawked at him, but others continued to stroll about, play games, or look at the exhibits. At home, and everywhere else he has traveled, Nixon is surrounded by the pomp, majesty, and power of the American Presidency. But among the ghosts of the thirteen Ming emperors, he was just another man with a long nose and a brown coat.

The unruly herd of U.S. reporters and television people drew some attention from people in the streets. They looked with wonder at our funny clothes and exotic equipment. But many passersby paid us no heed at all. Some went out of their way to avoid us. A few wide-eyed little children were whisked away from the "foreign devils" by their mothers.

CBS anchorman Walter Cronkite drew a throng of fans to the airport in Guam, a U.S. territory, on his way to Peking. But in China he passed unrecognized—perhaps the only country in the world where that can happen. The day President and Mrs. Nixon visited the Great Wall, Cronkite and Barbara Walters of NBC strayed too far up the Wall. When they tried to return to their car, they found their way barred by Chinese security men. In his rich baritone, Cronkite lectured the Chinese: "I am Walter Cronkite, and this is Miss Walters. We have to get to our car." The Chinese didn't budge; Walter's magic didn't work in China.

American girls in the party made no special impression

on Chinese men, somewhat to their annoyance. Connie Gerrard, a pretty White House secretary, complained, "They looked at me as if I was a rice paddy." The Pan American stewardesses on the press plane, in their trim uniforms and short skirts, also drew no admiring glances at the Shanghai airport. Stewardess Amanda Hamilton pouted that the Chinese soldiers "didn't look at my legs the way American soldiers would. What's the matter with my legs?" [Editor's note: nothing.]

A Chinese-speaking foreigner asked a worker in Peking if he thought Mrs. Nixon was pretty. The answer was that he couldn't tell because she looked so different from Chinese women.

Americans who have traveled in the Soviet Union or Eastern Europe are used to being asked countless questions about their clothes, their cars, their homes, their wages, and way of life. There was almost none of that in China. People just didn't seem interested.

While the Nixon visit rattled chanceries and dominated headlines and TV screens around the world, it was almost lost among the vast multitudes of China. People were aware of it, but it didn't seem to matter especially. Nixon was here, they seemed to be saying by their reaction, but he will be gone tomorrow, and it won't mean much in the way we eat or work or live.

Once again, as so many times before, immemorial China had swallowed up an invading army.

"A HELL OF A STORY"

BY CHARLES W. BAILEY

The tall, thin Chinese stepped to the microphone at the front of the auditorium, cleared his throat and began: "The Chinese side is responsible for the administration and management of the press. If the American officials wish to use this press center for a press conference they are requested to raise the point with the information department of the Foreign Ministry—and we will consider it."

There was a small ripple of laughter—slightly nervous laughter—from the hundred-odd American journalists seated in the brand-new press center. They had just landed in Peking ("Peking, *China*, for God's sake," one reporter kept saying to himself) on what they already knew was the oddest assignment of their careers.

The next seven days in China proved them right beyond their wildest dreams. In the process, the Nixon visit emerged as an exercise in the uses, misuses, and abuses of late twentieth-century journalism.

The invasion of China by the massed American press began to take shape in July 1971 when Chou En-lai agreed to receive Nixon. Talking secretly then to Henry Kissinger, Chou suggested that the People's Republic would find it difficult to accommodate the kind of press party that normally traveled abroad with the President. Perhaps, he suggested, it would be enough to send ten writers and a couple of camera crews.

Thus began a negotiating process that took on a life of its own within the larger negotiation between Chou and Nixon. The number of press to be allowed into China gradually crept up: to twenty-eight, to eighty, finally (a week before the trip began) to eighty-seven. It was, at any of these figures, agonizingly small. The White House received more than 2,000 applications—and while most of these came from news organizations whose claim, if any, to a place on the list was easily dismissed, press secretary Ronald Ziegler still had several hundred requests from major news organizations that covered his boss every day—and that shaped the perceptions of an electorate that in less than a year would decide whether Nixon would spend another four years in the White House.

Beyond the mere matter of numbers there were other problems for Ziegler. The networks wanted to broadcast live from China and the technical problems involved would be staggering. At the time planning began, communications from Peking to the outside world consisted of a few radio channels of dubious quality. The first White House suggestion was to turn a Boeing 747 jumbo jet into a mobile broadcasting studio by cramming it with equipment, parking it at Peking Airport, and using it to send TV signals up to the mid-Pacific communications satellite. This idea was vetoed by the Chinese: it would, they said, be an infringement on their sovereignty to have a foreign country broadcasting from their soil. Instead they would consider building—*and* operating—a broadcast facility that would feed TV, radio, telephone, and teletype signals into a portable ground station which *they* would lease and operate. (Throughout the process of preparing and carrying out the visit, the Chinese were meticulous about preserving their sovereignty, whether the issue was as large as a ground station or as small as whether a press bus could leave at a particular time. Once the Americans got used to the idea, it created few problems; but for a White House used to having its way abroad as at home, it took some getting used to.) The White House happened to have a plan for a two-story broadcast building, and gave it to the Chinese. A few weeks later word came from Peking that the building was going up and that the government of the People's Republic was leasing a ground station from Western Union International.

With that big hurdle behind it, the White House began to pare the pile of press applications to fit the limit negotiated with the Chinese. In the end, it came out about the way most Washington newsmen figured it would. The big three networks got the lion's share: twelve correspondents (including all the Big Names) and twenty-five cameramen and producers (three of whom turned out to be network vice presidents). Public Broadcasting, by contrast, got one correspondent, no cameramen. The two big wire services got three reporters and two photographers each. There were six magazine writers, four radio broadcasters, two magazine photographers, two photo darkroom technicians, twenty-one newspaper reporters, three syndicated columnists (selected to represent a left-to-right spectrum), and a man from the Voice of America.

They paid their way with hard work—for some, the hardest work they had ever done, thanks to the scatter-gun nature of the story and the peculiarities of deadlines skewed by the time difference between Peking and Peoria. Everyone (except for those network vice-presidents, who managed to find a good deal of time for shopping) was busy twenty hours of each day.

The pressure was heightened by the reporters' own desire to see as much as they could in the little time they had—and by the fact that the Chinese obligingly offered a bewildering variety of tours and visits to fill the time—it was, in fact, most of the time all week—when Nixon and Chou were talking to each other behind closed doors. Reporters could watch lung operations or caesarian sections—and talk to the patients. They could visit universities and auto plants and communes and neighborhood committees and museums and the People's Liberation Army and nurseries and schools of all varieties. With a little effort, reporters could make arrangements for other visits as well. And there was nothing (except the pressure of time, the language barrier, and the understandable reluctance of the Chinese to lose track of the reporters) to prevent them from wandering off on their own.

What resulted was a massive outpouring of words and pictures. The focus—and the quality—was varied. Television sent back the spectacles (banquets, ballet, the Great Wall, scenic Hangchow, the Ming Tombs). The wire services, as is their custom, filed one new lead after another in an effort to outdo each other. Most newspaper writers tried to pull the main story together each day and also file "color" and interpretive pieces. Many reporters, particularly those who had worked in Communist countries before, were wary of instant analysis. Others were not. One of the wary ones was infuriated when, on the *second* day of the visit, his editor complained that some of his colleagues seemed to be getting out and talking to "ordinary Chinese people," and suggested he provide some of the same kind of story. The "ordinary" Chinese, of course, were the government interpreters and party cadres and carefully briefed hosts at communes and factory tours who were the only Chinese most reporters had time or opportunity to meet.

If there was a single dominant feeling among the visiting U.S. reporters, it was frustration. There was so much to do, so little time to do it. For those who had worked in China in the old days, and for those others who had spent years studying the new China from outside, it was especially frustrating; for these men, the presence of the President, and the requirement that his activities be reported, was almost an irritating distraction. Everyone wanted to stay longer (though when the Chinese finally said no to all but two of the applicants, the rest—by then exhausted—were for the most part rather relieved) and most want to return. China turned out to be every bit as good a story as they expected—and then some.

But there was another side to the communications story— a Chinese side—and in the long run it may turn out to be the most important aspect of the Nixon visit. The American visitors had an impact on China that of course cannot yet be measured with any certainty, but which clearly went far beyond the immediate contact between the visiting journalists and the few people they met.

For one thing, the Chinese government gave the visit big billing. Once they decided to tell their people Nixon was there, the Chinese leaders told everyone—and in a big way via newspapers and radio and bulletin boards and on the limited television facilities.

Second, the Chinese government found out that it could, when it wished and when it put its mind to it, handle a substantial number of foreign correspondents at once. The visiting White House press group was three times the size of the permanent resident Western press corps in Peking; it was also far and away the biggest group of journalists ever allowed into the P.R.C. at once. The Americans came away with a feeling—something less than certainty but more than mere wishful thinking—that it will be easier for U.S. reporters to gain admission to China in the future. Indeed, the discovery by the Chinese that they could deal with so large a group of visiting journalists may well have played a role in their willingness to commit themselves, in the final communiqué, to future exchanges of newsmen with the United States.

Perhaps the most significant development arising from the press coverage of the Nixon trip was the decision of the Chinese to buy and install permanently in Shanghai a satellite ground station of their own. This was a unilateral decision; though the White House expressed concern about communications out of Shanghai, it was by all accounts the Chinese who thought of acquiring the additional transmitter. More important than its use during the Nixon visit, of course, is the fact that unlike the rented unit in Peking it will remain in place and in operation. Again, one cannot measure the impact on China of being thus permanently linked to the rest of the world by an instantaneous communications system; but installation of the Shanghai station has to be read as a decision by the country's leaders to enlarge their contacts with the rest of the world—the very process Nixon wanted to encourage by his visit.

A great many words (though not as many as the experts expected) were broadcast or written from China during Nixon's journey. Some were informed, others misinformed or uninformed. Some were naive, some cynical. Some will turn out to be prescient; others will look foolish a month or a year from now, if indeed they have not already been proven wrong.

The American press in China found itself playing an unaccustomed role: it was, as Nixon and Kissinger both said in differing contexts during the visit, a part of the process of diplomacy and not merely an observer of that process. It was not a comfortable role for most of the American reporters who went with Nixon; but it was just one more anomaly on an assignment that was without precedent in American journalism.

P.S. It was a hell of a story, too.

CONCLUSION

BY RICHARD WILSON

"The week that changed the world" began in doubt. It was a journey into the unknown. The advance planning of the President, Dr. Henry A. Kissinger, and Secretary of State William P. Rogers had an open end. The way was lined with booby traps and pitfalls. But the President stumbled into none of them and emerged at the end in formal agreement with the People's Republic of China on broadened relations which he deems to be of historic proportions.

At what price? The price, according to some, was a sellout of the Republic of China on Taiwan to gain agreement with the once implacable enemy on the mainland. Others considered the agreement no sellout at all, but a recognition of the objective reality that Taiwan is, in fact, relatively secure in the atmosphere of reduced tension created by President Nixon's agreement with the mainland Chinese leadership.

In the longer run of history, others thought, the ultimate significance will lie in the two joint appearances of President Nixon and Premier Chou En-lai at banquets in the Great Hall of the People in Peking. These appearances in the seat of power of what once was called Communist China, and before the whole world via satellite-borne television, symbolized the central fact that the new China and the United States had decided to let agreement on some practical matters override the bristling ideological hostility of the past twenty years. Chou pledged "unswerving" support of that idea. Nixon pledged his country to carry out its part of the bargain in the same spirit.

The visit itself was both the medium and the message. The fact that it took place at all, and in colorful and dramatic circumstances from beginning to end without a serious bobble or hitch, was the significant major news event. The ultimate meaning of the great scenes in Peking, Hangchow, and Shanghai may be clouded.

But the immediate impact tends to support President Nixon's analysis, stated at a farewell banquet in Shanghai, that "this was the week that changed the world." The tremors of change were felt first in Tokyo, Taipei, Saigon, New Delhi, and Moscow, where the shape of the new Asia is being forged.

All those capitals were given notice that President Nixon and Premier Chou En-lai do not accept the idea that any single nation, including China, the United States, and Russia, can hold sway over all Asia. No spheres of influence. No hegemony. If this proves in fact to be the reality, the power struggle in Asia that has endangered the peace of the world will be coming to its end.

How plausible is that idea? More plausible by far than when President Nixon descended from *The Spirit of '76*, to be received with cool correctness by Chou En-lai at Peking airport. A slow chill spread through the Nixon party. On a brilliant, sunny day of midwinter, the populace of Peking ignored President Nixon's presence. The Communist hierarchy was turned out to greet him. The people were not. Was this to be the tone of the Nixon visit?

The chill was dispelled when President Nixon was immediately taken to the residence of Chairman Mao Tse-tung for an hour's discussion. From then on, the Nixon meetings focused on the hard differences of Chinese-American policy and how they might be bridged.

In the end they were not bridged. They were acknowledged and defined and catalogued. They were brought out for the world to see in concise and hard terms. Delicacies of international talk were swept away. Half the effort of Dr. Henry A. Kissinger, in long sessions with his Chinese opposites, was devoted to defining the differences. Defining the agreements was easier.

The communiqué that finally emerged must go down in diplomatic annals as the authoritative definition of Chinese-American relations, as the two countries began the long process of improving them.

In advance, the Chinese were expected to agree to cultural, people-to-people exchanges and means of developing trade. These were duly recorded in the final communiqué. One of the most important of the agreements was not mentioned in the communiqué at all. What President Nixon described as a "communications belt" is to set in motion to establish regular contacts between representatives of the United States and China. This continuing contact was compared to the nonproductive ambassadorial talks that have been going on in Warsaw for two decades on solving mutual questions growing out of the Korean War. A "contact point" is to be established in Ottawa, or some other capital where the Chinese People's Republic has diplomatic representation.

However unproductive the talks in Warsaw, they served as a contact point for feeling out the Chinese more than a year ago on the prospective Nixon visit. In the future the new contact point could serve a useful purpose also in matters growing out of the China visit.

But the way ahead is hard. Let there be no doubt of the dedicated, selfless, statusless nature of the Chinese Communist society. Part of this was deliberately revealed to the traveling press, as recounted elsewhere in this book. The Chinese that the press saw and talked with in communes, hospitals, factories, universities, and neighborhood groups were imbued with a superior knowledge of truth. They were possessed with the doctrines of Mao as the religiously devout in America are possessed by the spirit of Christ. There is no doubt. The Chinese speak of "our great leader, Chairman Mao" as unaffectedly as a pious Christian speaks of "our Savior."

A people thus indoctrinated with truth can, as Premier Chou did, speak of the zigzags of history as unimportant. The Chinese truth will prevail and all the world will one day recognize it. In that spirit the Chinese could enter into a compact with the devil. That compact would lead to peace and friendship all over the world, Chinese-style, according to the Maoist view.

The Chinese society is one of hard work, low pay, and discipline—a far cry from the concepts of the Mao cultists among the young in the United States. It is a society, it has been said, where the universities are run to suit Abbie Hoffman, with enough law and order to satisfy Spiro Agnew.

Because the dedication runs so deep, wishful ideas about people-to-people contacts and cultural exchanges changing the atmosphere can be accepted as desirable, but with minimum promise of altering the course of history. The President made it clear that he knows this. But he bargained hard for a beginning that would not only send Americans to China but bring Chinese to America. In the same way, he bargained for trade relationships, knowing well enough that for many years the Chinese and Americans cannot exchange a very large volume of goods.

The prospects for formal diplomatic relationships were probably improved. The British are still waiting for ambassadorial exchange, and we are likely to wait for some time also. China is emerging slowly into the whole world, still bemused by its exalted status as the Middle Kingdom of enlightenment and wisdom.

This was the China seen by those who accompanied Nixon. Deeply involved, several times into the early hours of the morning at the highest power level, Nixon may have seen less of the façade of China than those who accompanied him and who were escorted to many places where Mao doctrine is pure and safe to expose to Western eyes. This was a missionary effort by the Chinese. They were leading the benighted Westerners into enlightenment, as a couple of generations ago the American missionaries tried to lead the heathen Chinese into a state of grace.

So what does it all add up to?

First, Nixon went to China and was received with unfailing courtesy and respect.

Second, the Chinese permitted more Westerners to see more of China in a shorter period of time than would have been thought conceivable a year ago.

Third, Nixon found a formula involving terms of reference about Taiwan different than in the past, which made it possible to define a limited agreement with China after twenty years of hostility and confrontation.

Fourth, there were concessions by the Chinese as well as the United States, which at the very least breaks the stalemate in Chinese-American relations.

Fifth, Chou and Mao have agreed to permit the isolated Chinese to visit the United States and expose themselves to Western thought, of which the young Chinese are largely unaware. When they come, Americans will find them to be formidable, intellectual competitors, as well as vigorous opponents in ping-pong and badminton.

And, finally, communications have been opened up with China on a continuing, and perhaps halting, basis. But the beginning was made and no one who accompanied the President can say with certainty where it will eventually lead.

Only Nixon, with his credentials of anticommunism reaching back into the 1940s, could have carried America so far along this road.

TEXTS OF OFFICIAL
STATEMENTS

PREMIER CHOU EN-LAI'S TOAST AT THE BANQUET IN HONOR OF PRESIDENT NIXON
FEBRUARY 21, 1972

Mr. President and Mrs. Nixon. Ladies and gentlemen, comrades and friends.

First of all, I have the pleasure on behalf of Chairman Mao Tse-tung and the Chinese Government to extend our welcome to Mr. President and Mrs. Nixon and to our other American guests.

I also wish to take this opportunity to extend on behalf of the Chinese people cordial greetings to the American people on the other side of the great ocean.

President Nixon's visit to our country at the invitation of the Chinese Government provides the leaders of the two countries with an opportunity of meeting in person to seek the normalization of relations between the two countries and also to exchange views on questions of concern to the two sides.

This is a positive move in conformity with the desire of the Chinese and American people and an event unprecedented in the history of relations between China and the United States.

The American people are a great people. The Chinese people are a great people. The peoples of our two countries have always been friendly to each other. But owing to reasons known to all, contacts between the two peoples were suspended for over twenty years.

Now, through the common efforts of China and the United States, the gates to friendly contact have finally been opened.

At the present time it has become a strong desire of the Chinese and American people to promote the normalization of relations between the two countries and work for the relaxation of tension. The people and the people alone are the motive force in the making of world history. We are confident that the day will surely come when this common desire of our two peoples will be realized.

The social systems of China and the United States are fundamentally different and there exist great differences between the Chinese Government and the United States Government. However, these differences should not hinder China and the United States from establishing normal state relations on the basis of the five principles of mutual respect for sovereignty and territorial integrity; mutual non-aggression; noninterference in each other's internal affairs; equality and mutual benefit, and peaceful coexistence. Still less should they lead to war.

As early as 1955 the Chinese Government publicly stated that the Chinese people do not want to have a war with the United

States and that the Chinese Government is willing to sit down and enter into negotiations with the United States Government. This is a policy which we have pursued consistently. We have taken note of the fact that in his speech before setting out for China, President Nixon, on his part, said that "what we must do is to find a way to see that we can have differences without being enemies in war."

We hope that, through a frank exchange of views between our two sides, to gain a clearer notion of our differences and make efforts to find common grounds, a new start can be made in the relations between our two countries.

In conclusion I propose a toast to the health of President Nixon and Mrs. Nixon, to the health of our other American guests, to the health of all our friends and comrades present and to the friend-ships between the Chinese and American people.

PRESIDENT NIXON'S TOAST
AT THE BANQUET HOSTED BY
PREMIER CHOU EN-LAI
FEBRUARY 21, 1972

Mr. Prime Minister and all of your distinguished guests this evening:

On behalf of all of your American guests, I wish to thank you for the incomparable hospitality for which the Chinese people are justly famous throughout the world. I particularly want to pay tribute, not only to those who prepared the magnificent dinner, but also to those who have provided the splendid music. Never have I heard American music played better in a foreign land.

Mr. Prime Minister, I wish to thank you for your very gracious and eloquent remarks. At this very moment, through the wonder of telecommunications, more people are seeing and hearing what we say than on any other such occasion in the whole history of the world. Yet, what we say here will not be long remembered. What we do here can change the world.

As you said in your toast, the Chinese people are a great people, the American people are a great people. If our two people are enemies, the future of this world we share together is dark indeed. But if we can find common ground to work together, the chance for world peace is immeasurably increased.

In the spirit of frankness which I hope will characterize our talks this week, let us recognize at the outset these points: We have at times in the past been enemies. We have great differences today. What brings us together is that we have common interests which transcend those differences. As we discuss our differences, neither of us will compromise our principles. But while we cannot close the gulf between us, we can try to bridge it so that we may be able to talk across it.

So, let us, in these next five days, start a long march together, not in lockstep, but on different roads leading to the same goal, the goal of building a world structure of peace and justice in which all may stand together with equal dignity and in which each nation, large or small, has a right to determine its own form of government, free of outside interference or domination. The world watches. The world listens. The world waits to see what we will do. What is the world? In a personal sense, I think of my eldest daughter whose birthday is today. As I think of her, I think of all the children in the world, in Asia, in Africa, in Europe, in the Americas, most of whom were born since the date of the foundation of the People's Republic of China.

What legacy shall we leave our children? Are they destined to die for the hatreds which have plagued the old world, or are they destined to live because we had the vision to build a new world?

There is no reason for us to be enemies. Neither of us seeks the territory of the other; neither of us seeks domination over the other; neither of us seeks to stretch out our hands and rule the world.

Chairman Mao has written, "So many deeds cry out to be done, and always urgently. The world rolls on. Time passes. Ten thousand years are too long. Seize the day, seize the hour."

This is the hour. This is the day for our two peoples to rise to the heights of greatness which can build a new and a better world.

In that spirit, I ask all of you present to join me in raising your glasses to Chairman Mao, to Prime Minister Chou, and to the friendship of the Chinese and American people which can lead to friendship and peace for all people in the world.

JOINT COMMUNIQUE
FEBRUARY 28, 1972
SHANGHAI, PEOPLE'S REPUBLIC OF CHINA

President Richard Nixon of the United States of America visited the People's Republic of China at the invitation of Premier Chou En-lai of the People's Republic of China from February 21 to February 28, 1972. Accompanying the President were Mrs. Nixon, U.S. Secretary of State William Rogers, Assistant to the President Dr. Henry Kissinger, and other American officials.

President Nixon met with Chairman Mao Tse-tung of the Communist Party of China on February 21. The two leaders had a serious and frank exchange of views on Sino-U.S. relations and world affairs.

During the visit, extensive, earnest and frank discussions were held between President Nixon and Premier Chou En-lai on the normalization of relations between the United States of America and the People's Republic of China, as well as on other matters of interest to both sides. In addition, Secretary of State William

Rogers and Foreign Minister Chi Peng-fei held talks in the same spirit.

President Nixon and his party visited Peking and viewed cultural, industrial and agricultural sites, and they also toured Hangchow and Shanghai where, continuing discussions with Chinese leaders, they viewed similar places of interest.

The leaders of the People's Republic of China and the United States of America found it beneficial to have this opportunity, after so many years without contact, to present candidly to one another their views on a variety of issues. They reviewed the international situation in which important changes and great upheavals are taking place and expounded their respective positions and attitudes.

The U.S. side stated: Peace in Asia and peace in the world require efforts both to reduce immediate tensions and to eliminate the basic causes of conflict. The United States will work for a just and secure peace: just, because it fulfills the aspirations of peoples and nations for freedom and progress; secure, because it removes the danger of foreign aggression. The United States supports individual freedom and social progress for all the peoples of the world, free of outside pressure or intervention. The United States believes that the effort to reduce tensions is served by improving communication between countries that have different ideologies so as to lessen the risks of confrontation through accident, miscalculation or misunderstanding. Countries should treat each other with mutual respect and be willing to compete peacefully, letting performance be the ultimate judge. No country should claim infallibility and each country should be prepared to reexamine its own attitudes for the common good. The United States stressed that the peoples of Indochina should be allowed to determine their destiny without outside intervention; its constant primary objective has been a negotiated solution; the eight-point proposal put forward by the Republic of Vietnam and the United States on January 27, 1972 represents a basis for the attainment of that objective; in the absence of a negotiated settlement, the United States envisages the ultimate withdrawal of all U.S. forces from the region consistent with the aim of self-determination for each country of Indochina. The United States will maintain its close ties with and support for the Republic of Korea; the United States will support efforts of the Republic of Korea to seek a relaxation of tension and increased communication in the Korean peninsula. The United States places the highest value of its friendly relations with Japan; it will continue to develop the existing close bonds. Consistent with the United Nations Security Council resolution of December 21, 1971, the United States favors the continuation of the cease-fire between India and Pakistan and the withdrawal of all military forces to within their own territories and to their own sides of the cease-fire line in Jammu and Kashmir; the United States supports the right of the peoples of South Asia to shape their own future in peace, free of military threat, and without having the area become the subject of great power rivalry.

The Chinese side stated: Wherever there is oppression, there is resistance. Countries want independence, nations want liberation and the people want revolution—this has become the irresistible trend of history. All nations, big or small, should be equal; big nations should not bully the small and strong nations should not bully the weak. China will never be a superpower and it opposes hegemony and power politics of any kind. The Chinese side stated that it firmly supports the struggles of all the oppressed people and nations for freedom and liberation and that the people of all countries have the right to choose their social systems according to their own wishes and the right to safeguard the independence, sovereignty and territorial integrity of their own countries and oppose foreign aggression, interference, control and subversion. All foreign troops should be withdrawn to their own countries.

The Chinese side expressed its firm support to the peoples of Vietnam, Laos and Cambodia in their efforts for the attainment of their goal and its firm support to the seven-point proposal of the Provisional Revolutionary Government of the Republic of South Vietnam and the elaboration of February this year on the two key problems in the proposal, and to the Joint Declaration of the Summit Conference of the Indochinese Peoples. It firmly supports the eight-point program for the peaceful unification of Korea put forward by the Government of the Democratic People's Republic of Korea on April 12, 1971, and the stand for the abolition of the "U.N. Commission for the Unification and Rehabilitation of Korea." It firmly opposes the revival and outward expansion of Japanese militarism and firmly supports the Japanese people's desire to build an independent, democratic, peaceful and neutral Japan. It firmly maintains that India and Pakistan should, in accordance with the United Nations resolutions on the India-Pakistan question, immediately withdraw all their forces to their respective territories and to their own sides of the cease-fire line in Jammu and Kashmir, and firmly supports the Pakistan Government and people in their struggle to preserve their independence and sovereignty and the people of Jammu and Kashmir in their struggle for the right of self-determination.

There are essential differences between China and the United States in their social systems and foreign policies. However, the two sides agreed that countries, regardless of their social systems, should conduct their relations on the principles of respect for the sovereignty and territorial integrity of all states, nonaggression against other states, noninterference in the internal affairs of other states, equality and mutual benefit, and peaceful coexistence. International disputes should be settled on this basis, without resorting to the use or threat of force. The United States and the People's Republic of China are prepared to apply these principles to their mutual relations.

With these principles of international relations in mind the two sides stated that:

- Progress toward the normalization of relations between China and the United States is in the interests of all countries.
- Both wish to reduce the danger of international military conflict,
- Neither should seek hegemony in the Asia-Pacific region and each is opposed to efforts by any other country or group of countries to establish such hegemony; and
- Neither is prepared to negotiate on behalf of any third party or to enter into agreements or understandings with the other directed at other states.

Both sides are of the view that it would be against the interests of the peoples of the world for any major country to collude with another against other countries, or for major countries to divide up the world into spheres of interest.

The two sides reviewed the long-standing serious disputes between China and the United States. The Chinese side reaffirmed its position: The Taiwan question is the crucial question obstructing the normalization of relations between China and the United States; the Government of the People's Republic of China is the sole legal government of China; Taiwan is a province of China which has long been returned to the motherland; the liberation of Taiwan is China's internal affair in which no other country has the right to interfere; and all U.S. forces and military installations must be withdrawn from Taiwan. The Chinese Government firmly opposes any activities which aim at the creation of "one China, one Taiwan," "one China, two governments," "two Chinas," and "independent Taiwan" or advocate that "the status of Taiwan remains to be determined."

The U.S. side declared: The United States acknowledges that all Chinese on either side of the Taiwan Strait maintain there is but one China and that Taiwan is a part of China. The United States Government does not challenge that position. It reaffiirms its interest in a peaceful settlement of the Taiwan question by the Chinese themselves. With this prospect in mind, it affirms the ultimate objective of the withdrawal of all U.S. forces and military installations from Taiwan. In the meantime, it will progressively reduce its forces and military installations on Taiwan as the tension in the area diminishes.

The two sides agreed that it is desirable to broaden the understanding between the two peoples. To this end, they discussed specific areas in such fields as science, technology, culture, sports and journalism, in which people-to-people contacts and exchanges would be mutually beneficial. Each side undertakes to facilitate the further development of such contacts and exchanges.

Both sides view bilateral trade as another area from which mutual benefit can be derived, and agreed that economic relations based on equality and mutual benefit are in the interest of the peoples of the two countries. They agree to facilitate the progressive development of trade between their two countries.

The two sides agreed that they will stay in contact through various channels, including the sending of a senior U.S. representative to Peking from time to time for concrete consultations to further the normalization of relations between the two countries and continue to exchange views on issues of common interest.

The two sides expressed the hope that the gains achieved during this visit would open up new prospects for the relations between the two countries. They believe that the normalization of relations between the two countries is not only in the interest of the Chinese and American peoples but also contributes to the relaxation of tension in Asia and the world.

President Nixon, Mrs. Nixon and the American party expressed their appreciation for the gracious hospitality shown them by the Government and people of the People's Republic of China.

THE PRESIDENT'S SPEECH
ON HIS RETURN HOME,
FEBRUARY 28, 1972

Mr. Vice President, members of the Congress, members of the Cabinet, members of the diplomatic corps, and ladies and gentlemen:

I want to express my very deep appreciation and the appreciation of all of us for this wonderfully warm welcome that you've given us and for the support that we have had on the trip that we just completed, from Americans of both political parties in all walks of life across this land.

And because of the superb efforts of the hard-working members of the press who accompanied us—they got even less sleep than I did—millions of Americans in this past week have seen more of China than I did.

Consequently, tonight, I would like to talk to you not about what we saw but about what we did, to sum up the results of the trip and to put it in perspective.

When I announced this trip last July, I described it as a journey for peace. In the last thirty years Americans have in three different wars gone off in the hundreds of thousands to fight and some to die, in Asia and in the Pacific.

One of the central motives behind my journey to China was to prevent that from happening a fourth time to another generation of Americans.

As I've often said, peace means more than the mere absence of war. In a technical sense we were at peace with the People's Republic of China before this trip. But a gulf of almost 12,000 miles and twenty-two years of noncommunication and hostility separated the United States of America from the 750 million people who live in the People's Republic of China—and that's one-fourth of all the people in the world.

As a result of this trip we have started the long process of building a bridge across that gulf, and even now we have something better than the mere absence of war.

Not only have we completed a week of intensive talks at the highest levels, we have set up a procedure whereby we can continue to have discussions in the future.

We have demonstrated that nations with very deep and fundamental differences can learn to discuss those differences calmly, rationally, and frankly without compromising their principles.

This is the basis of a structure for peace; where we can talk about differences rather than fight about them.

The primary goal of this trip was to reestablish communication with the People's Republic of China after a generation of hostility. We achieved that goal.

Let me turn now to our joint communiqué. We did not bring back any written or unwritten agreements that will guarantee peace in our time. We did not bring home any magic formula which will make unnecessary the efforts of the American people to continue to maintain the strength so that we can continue to be free.

We made some necessary and important beginnings, however, in several areas.

We entered into agreements to expand cultural, educational, and journalistic contacts between the Chinese and the American people.

We agreed to work to begin and broaden trade between our two countries.

We have agreed that the communications that have now been established between our Governments will be strengthened and expanded.

Most important, we have agreed on some rules of international conduct which will reduce the risk of confrontation and war in Asia and in the Pacific.

We agreed that we are opposed to domination of the Pacific area by any one power.

We agreed that international disputes be settled without the use of force, and we agreed that we are prepared to apply this principle to our mutual relations.

With respect to Taiwan, we stated our established policy that our forces overseas will be reduced gradually as tensions ease, and that our ultimate objective is to withdraw our forces as a peaceful settlement is achieved.

We've agreed that we will not negotiate the fate of other nations behind their back and we did not do so in Peking. There were no secret deals of any kind.

We have done all this without giving up any United States

commitment to any country.

In our talks—the talks that I had with the leaders of the People's Republic and that the Secretary of State had with the office of the Government of the People's Republic in the foreign affairs area—we both realized that a bridge of understanding that spans almost 12,000 miles and twenty-two years of hostility can't be built in one week of discussions, but we have agreed to begin to build that bridge, recognizing that our work will require years of patient effort.

We made no attempt to pretend that major differences did not exist between our two governments, because they do exist.

This communiqué was unique in honestly setting forth differences rather than trying to cover them up with diplomatic double-talk.

One of the gifts that we left behind in Hangchow was the planted sapling of the American redwood tree. As all Californians know, and as most Americans know, redwoods grow from saplings into giants of the forest. But the process is not one of days, or even years—it is a process of centuries.

Just as we hope that those saplings—those tiny saplings that we left in China—will grow one day into mighty redwoods, so we hope, too, that the seeds planted on this journey for peace will grow and prosper into a more enduring structure for peace and security in the Western Pacific.

But peace, peace is too urgent to wait for centuries. We must seize the moment to move toward that goal now, and this is what we have done on this journey.

As I am sure you realize, it was a great experience for us to see the timeless wonders of ancient China, the changes that are being made in modern China.

And one fact stands out among many others from my talks with the Chinese leaders. It is their total belief, their total dedication to their system of government. That is their right, just as it is the right of any country to choose the kind of government it wants.

But as I return from this trip, just as has been the case on my return from other trips abroad which have taken me to over eighty countries, I come back to America with an even stronger faith in our system of government.

As I flew across America today, all the way from Alaska, over the Rockies, the Plains, and then on to Washington, I thought of the greatness of our country.

And most of all, I thought of the freedom, the opportunity, the progress that 200 million Americans are privileged to enjoy.

I realized again, this is a beautiful country.

And tonight my prayer, and my hope, is that as a result of this trip our children will have a better chance to grow up in a peaceful world.

Thank you.

ABOUT THE PHOTOGRAPHERS

OLLIE ATKINS is personal photographer to President Richard M. Nixon. He was a photo journalist with the Birmingham *Post*, the Washington *Daily News* and the *Saturday Evening Post*. Mr. Atkins covered World War II and the Korean War, and also Europe, Japan, India and Africa. He became photographer to Mr. Nixon during the 1968 election campaign. He is a past president of the White House Photographers and is a member of the National Press Photographers Association.

BYRON SHUMAKER has been a photographer with the Department of the Interior since 1970 and frequently does special assignments for the White House. He started his photography career at *Life* and was a combat photographer with the U.S. Army. He was a news photographer for the Cincinnati *Post & Times-Star* and later the Washington *Evening Star*.

ABOUT THE WRITERS

CHARLES W. BAILEY is Associate Editor and Washington bureau chief of the *Minneapolis Tribune*. He is the coauthor of three books—*No High Ground, Seven Days in May,* and *Convention.* He is a former president of the White House Correspondents Association.

ROBERT S. BOYD joined the Washington bureau of Knight Newspapers in 1960. He has reported from almost every Communist country, including North Vietnam, and most Asian nations. He is the coauthor of a novel of political intrigue, *A Certain Evil.*

STAN CARTER is diplomatic correspondent of the *New York Daily News*. He covered the Korean War and named Heartbreak Ridge. Carter has been with the *Daily News* for ten years, first in New York interpreting foreign news, then in Washington, covering the White House and State Department.

BOB CONSIDINE's "On the Line" column for King Features Syndicate appears regularly in the nation's top newspapers. With William Randolph Hearst, Jr. and Frank Conniff, he was granted an exclusive interview with Nikita Khrushchev in Moscow in November 1957. For this, the triumvirate won the Overseas Press Club Award for the best reporting abroad. Mr. Considine is the author of many magazine articles and a number of best-selling books. Over the years Considine has won a number of awards for his journalism.

FRANK CORMIER joined the Associated Press in Chicago in 1951. He transferred to Associated Press's Washington bureau in 1954 and, after specializing in reporting economic affairs, became Associated Press's White House correspondent in 1962.

ROBERT L. KEATLEY is diplomatic correspondent for the *Wall Street Journal*. He has been with the *Journal* since 1959, reporting from San Francisco, New York, London, Tokyo, Hong Kong, and then Washington. He visited the People's Republic of China in summer, 1971, for five weeks.

PHILIP POTTER is the *Baltimore Sun*'s Washington bureau chief. He has reported from Asia on many occasions in the past twenty-five years, and is an expert in Asian affairs. Having known Chou En-lai personally, Mr. Potter has traveled widely in China.

R. H. SHACKFORD is foreign affairs reporter and news analyst for the Scripps-Howard Newspaper Alliance. Long before the Washington-Peking thaw, Shackford believed Americans should know more about what went on behind the Bamboo Curtain. In 1964, he pioneered by filing a continuing series of articles titled "Report on Red China" for Scripps-Howard newspaper readers. He spent two years in Hong Kong, and visited all the nations bordering China.

J. F. TERHORST has been a Washington correspondent for the *Detroit News* since 1957 and the chief of its Washington Bureau since 1961. He has covered every presidential trip abroad and major domestic trips since 1960, and has been on assignment in Europe, the Middle East, Asia, and Latin America. In addition to his coverage for the *News*, Mr. terHorst writes a column that is syndicated nationally by the North American Newspaper Alliance.

HELEN THOMAS joined United Press International in 1943 and began covering the White House in 1961. She was president of the Women's National Press Club in 1959–60, and was the first woman in the fifty-seven-year history of the White House Correspondents' Association to serve on the board of governors. Miss Thomas received the 1968 award for best newspaperwoman from the American Newspaper Women's Club.

RICHARD WILSON is the author of a syndicated Washington column distributed by the Des Moines Register and Tribune Syndicate and published in numerous newspapers. In order to concentrate full time on the column, he recently relinquished his administrative duties as chief of the Washington bureau of the Cowles Publications. Wilson has been awarded the Pulitzer Prize in journalism for distinguished reporting of national affairs.

A NOTE ON THIS BOOK

THE TEXT OF THIS BOOK IS SET IN 9 POINT CALEDONIA. THIS TYPEFACE WAS CREATED BY WILLIAM ADDISON DWIGGINS, A PREEMINENT AMERICAN TYPE AND BOOK DESIGNER. ITS NAME (WHICH IS THE ANCIENT NAME FOR WHAT IS NOW CALLED SCOTLAND) DENOTES THAT THE FACE WAS INTENDED TO HAVE A SCOTCH-ROMAN FLAVOR. A READABLE AND CHARMING FACE POSSESSING A GREAT DEAL OF WARMTH AND HOSPITALITY, CALEDONIA IS WELL PROPORTIONED AND HAS LITTLE CONTRAST BETWEEN THICK AND THIN LINES.

THE COMPOSITION FOR THE TEXT OF
THE PRESIDENT'S TRIP TO CHINA
IS BY AMERICAN TYPESETTING COMPANY.

THE COLOR ENGRAVINGS AND PRINTING
FOR THE COVER AND TEXT
ARE FROM REGENSTEINER PRESS.

THE COVER COATING
IS BY PAPER CONVERTING CORPORATION.

BINDING IS BY W. F. HALL PRINTING COMPANY.

PAPER WAS SUPPLIED BY THE MEAD CORPORATION
FOR THE COVER, AND BY
KIMBERLY-CLARK CORPORATION FOR THE TEXT.

THE BOOK WAS DESIGNED BY LEN LEONE
AND GERALD T. COUNIHAN.
